SECOND & EXPANDED EDITION

SPIRIT MUSCLE©

God's Gift to Enable You To Flow in the Holy Spirit

Answers to the Misconceptions About
Speaking in Tongues
That Limit Your Spiritual Strength

Jonathan Derrick Mathe

Unless otherwise noted, all Scripture verses are taken from the NKJV Bible translation.

First Edition, Printed in the United States of America - 2018
ISBN 978-0-9997921-0-0

Second Edition, Printed in the United States of America - 2024
ISBN 978-0-9997921-1-7

See the companion book: ***Baptism of the Spirit & Fire*** *– Receiving God's Power to Destroy the Works of Darkness*

Renaissance Roar Ministry - www.RenaissanceRoar.com
www.RevivalRoar.com
www.SpiritAndTruthSchool.com

Special discounts are available on quantity purchases by churches, ministries, and others. For details, contact the author/publisher at the website above.

Endorsements & Reviews

By far this is the best book on the gift of tongues I have ever read. I worked at a Christian bookstore for a couple of years and have read everything I could on the gifts of the Holy Spirit.

This book deals with just about every question, and every misconception, and thoughtfully brings to light the scripture to address them all. It shares really practical and beneficial ways to exercise this gift biblically, to grow personally, and to minister to others effectively. I was thankful that he also touched on the lack of attention we give to the gift of interpretation within the church. I felt like saying FINALLY, someone's talking about that!!!!!

The author addresses other aspects of the Holy Spirit's gifts as well, which I found really helpful. It's easy to read and to understand, it's humorous at times and honest, and ***I found I couldn't put it down.*** Whether you're newly saved, exploring the teachings on the Holy Spirit, or have been walking with the Lord in this for a long time, this is a great resource. ***I highly recommend this book!***

- Stephanie H. (Amazon Reviewer)

After digging deep into this subject for a number of years to find the actual truth, ***I can say without a doubt, this is the best and most complete work on this subject that I have found.*** Most have a lot of "hand-waving" & Christianese, requiring you to do some ignoring of the facts in Scripture. This does not lead to sound reasoning and a paradigm based on the evidence.

For those of us who have been raised with a "disbelief" in tongues, as well as other spiritual gifts, ***this book lays out the evidence of scripture in an intelligent, coherent, and reasonable manner.*** The only really open & honest conclusion to Jonathan's teaching that I can imagine is, "Yup, there it is!"

- Mark C. (Amazon Reviewer)

This book is the most thorough book on tongues I have read. It answers all the important questions on tongues. The book is easy to understand, and I have bought several copies for my friends and family. It is my go-to book for anyone asking me about how to connect to the Holy Spirit.
I definitely recommend it.

- Michelle (Amazon Reviewer)

This book was FULL of helpful information! ***I finished the book in one afternoon*** because it was interesting, informative, easy to follow, and very helpful.

- Vicky B. (Amazon Reviewer)

Spirit Muscle is such a great book and the author does a wonderful job explaining the how & whys of this gift. I know there are many differing opinions on who can receive certain gifts so if you have been told that the gift of tongues is only for certain people then *Spirit Muscle* is for you.

- Denise L. (Amazon Reviewer)

I love this book! I have already given away four copies and am ordering five more. Jonathan Derrick Mathe lays out the importance of the gifts of tongues and why there seems to be so much confusion over the "least" of the gifts.

- Mark B. (Amazon Reviewer)

For a small book on the manifestation of spiritual 'tongues', I found this book to cover a lot of ground! It examines the 'what's', the 'why's', and the 'how's'. It looks at tongues in a supernaturally effective Christian life: both roots to the fruits. It is theological, practical, and personal. It's gracious and challenging. This book stays in touch with those values that are common to Christians from any tradition who are hungry for a lifetime of spiritual growth.

Pastor Steve Sorensen
BS Biola University; M.A.C.E and M.Div. Talbot Seminary; Masters Wagner University. JPL Church, Rancho Mirage, CA

About the Author

Jonathan travels nationally and internationally, serving as a church leader, itinerant minister, conference speaker, author, entrepreneur, and consultant to churches and ministries. He mentors churches, fellowships, and leaders throughout the nations to transition from traditional non-Spirit-filled church paradigms into vibrant, biblical outpourings of the Holy Spirit, life, and power that embrace Kingdom values.

A lover of truth, sincerity, and authenticity, he is a passionate prophetic teacher & preacher of the Word spending most of his time relationally serving churches; locally, regionally, and internationally, by helping to awaken, prepare, and equip God's people to enter into all the fullness of Salvation and to see Christ fully formed in His Church, with the demonstration of the Spirit and power, while adhering to healthy spiritual and character foundations.

He and his wife, Jessy, lead Renaissance Roar, an apostolic resource ministry-equipping center called to promote Revival & Reformation that results in the long-term, sustainable transformation of individuals, churches, cities, and nations.

He accomplishes this by hosting ***Spirit & Truth Schools***, which are ministry-equipping seminars that cover a broad array of ministry: supernatural power, prayer, spiritual gifts, healing, deliverance, the prophetic, five-fold leadership, etc., with power, effectiveness, understanding, wisdom, and biblical accuracy.

Jonathan is a member of the Apostolic Council for Freedom Crusades International and has a B.A. degree in International Business from San Diego State University, as well as a corporate managerial and entrepreneurial background. He is a husband and father to two children and resides in Southern California.

Spirit & Truth Schools

Ministry Equipping Seminars

A Spirit & Truth School is a four-session seminar held in a local church or a regional gathering of fellowships to introduce and/or strengthen topical ministry strategies that train, equip, and empower leaders and all believers to begin effectively doing the work of the specific ministry.

Converts or Disciples?: You Must Be Born-Again: Salvation, Baptism, & the Gospel

The Holy Spirit: A Promise or A Problem? Addressing the Objections That Hinder God from Moving in Your Life & Church

Power From On High: Receiving & Administering the Baptism of the Holy Spirit

How to Walk & Flow in the Spirit: Exchanging Good Ministry for God Ministry by Understanding Soul vs. Spirit

The Spirit of God Conference: All 3 of the *Holy Spirit* Seminars, in a conference.

Healing School 1: I'm Sick and I Want to Be Healed! - Now What?

Healing School 2: How To Minister Divine Healing

Fear No Evil: Demons, Curses, & Biblical Deliverance

Prayer That Moves Mountains: How to Pray Powerfully & Effectively - The First Step to Partnering with God for Revival

God's Government: Understanding the 5-fold Ministries as the 4 Pillars of the New Wineskin Church

The Perfect Church Renaissance: This Era When Revival, Awakening, & Reformation Converge for the Restoration of All Things Before the Return of Jesus Christ

www.RenaissanceRoar.com
www.RevivalRoar.com
www.SpiritAndTruthSchool.com

Table of Contents

Answers You'll Get if You Read This Book

Some **myths & misunderstandings** about speaking in tongues that will be answered in this book are:

- Tongues have ceased and are not needed today.
- The purpose of speaking in tongues was for the preaching of the Gospel.
- Tongues must be in a known human language.
- All tongues must be interpreted.
- There is no such thing as tongues as a "prayer language".
- Tongues are not needed any longer because we have the Bible.
- Tongues are just emotionally driven gibberish.
- You must speak in tongues to be saved.
- Tongues are not evidence of being full of the Holy Spirit.
- Speaking in tongues is a "lesser gift".
- You should only speak in tongues when the Holy Spirit leads.
- There is only one type of speaking in tongues.
- It is not the person who is speaking in tongues, but it is the Holy Spirit doing it, as the person is not in control.
- If God wants me to have the gift, He'll just give it to me.
- Speaking in Tongues manifests automatically when the believer receives the baptism of the Holy Spirit if God has ordained them to have the gift.
- Not every Christian can speak in tongues.

Chapter One

From Wimps to Warriors... An Introduction

The "97-pound weakling... Who became 'America's Most Perfectly Developed Man'"

I don't like bullies. It seems that bullying is getting a lot of attention these days, and rightly so.

From childhood, I remember an old cartoon advertisement that used to be in comic books starting in the 1930s and continuing for fifty years afterward. The ad was for Charles Atlas - the "97-pound weakling... Who became America's Most Perfectly Developed Man." All of the ads would feature different scenes of skinny, scrawny guys being picked on or pushed around by bigger men in various life situations: at the beach, on the street, on the dance floor, etc. And always, a girlfriend was watching and commenting on how she did not feel protected by her beau because he was such a weakling. After each incident, the skinny guy would get hold of

Charles Atlas's workout booklet and put it to use. In the next scene, you would see the transformed "He-Man" with his new muscles, punching out the bully to the delight and admiration of his girlfriend. Charles Atlas' promise was, "Let Me Give You a Body that Men Respect and Women Admire!"

The truth these ads would target was that every man had access to, and the ability to attain, that desired muscular physique, but they did not have the "know-how." Charles Atlas's workout guaranteed that they would get those muscles (and the respect, confidence, and admiration that came with them) if they consistently applied his workout techniques.

In the same way, we followers of Jesus Christ have access to, and the ability to attain, that "muscular spiritual physique"—*spirit muscle*—that will enable us to spread the Gospel of the Kingdom with the accompanying works and power of Jesus that should attest to the Message's authenticity. Every son and daughter of God is expected to walk as did the Firstborn Son, destroying the works of the devil (a bully), setting captives free, healing the broken-hearted, and bringing hope and good news…

PUTTING SPIRITUAL BULLIES IN THEIR PLACE!

To help equip us for this epic call, the Father has provided "every good and perfect gift" that we need to prepare for and carry out the mission effectively. If you will be open to His tools and His ways—His workout—then you too will be the "97-pound spiritual weakling… Who became the Kingdom's Most Perfectly Developed Disciple." Thus, allowing God to fulfill His money-back guarantee of, "Let Me Give You A Spirit that Gives Men Hope and the Devil Fears!"

Getting Spiritually "Ripped".... No Pain, No Gain

Just know that to build muscle, you first must rip or tear it down through stress and strain, and then it builds itself back up, bigger and stronger than before. There will be many parts of this book that will challenge you and everything that you believe to be true. If *how* I have written is offensive, then I apologize in advance, as that is the shortcoming on which I am working. But if *what* I have written is offensive to you, then a heart-check is helpful to make you aware of possible existing spiritual prejudices that would hinder your receptivity. The truth can be offensive, especially if you don't want to know it. Ask the Lord for His guidance and confirmation of specific things that are presented. He *will* answer because I know that He is faithful and that He desires us to walk in Spirit and in Truth more than we want it for ourselves!

Why This Book?

In my years of teaching and equipping the Body of Christ, I am often astounded at the level of misunderstanding that is pervasive in a large part of our Western Church regarding the working of the Holy Spirit, especially regarding receiving the baptism of the Holy Spirit, and in particular, the gift of speaking in tongues. What is also perplexing, yet not to the same degree, is the lack of solid, clear teaching put forth by those who do have the experience and a lifestyle of flowing in this gift.

There are numerous online teachings on this subject via YouTube and podcasts; some are good, but most are horrendously flawed (in fact, I think that my ears are still bleeding from the pain of those YouTube videos that I watched last night). What I see as the main failure of the majority of the teachings out there regarding the baptism of the Holy Spirit (B.O.T.H.S.) and tongues is that the teachings are *opinions* espoused by leaders/pastors who have neither received the BOTHS nor have they ever entered into exercising the gift of speaking in tongues. Simply stated, it is all *theoretical* to them, which is easily boiled down to teaching from *a lack of first-hand experience*.

There are many times that I have watched television documentaries on Jesus, the Bible, or biblically related topics, on television channels such as A&E, Discovery, History Channel, etc. Without fail, these documentaries will always have, if not multiple, Doctors or Professors of Theology from some well-known university or seminary, such as Harvard School of Divinity, and the like. As I watch them "shed light" on the given topic, giving their "expert and educated" opinion, I have found myself repeatedly saying, "I don't think this guy even knows the Lord." Out of the overflow of the heart, the mouth speaks. It is so clear as they talk about a *historical* Jesus that they have never met Him, the Living Christ.

In the same manner, as I listen to numerous teachings on these supernatural topics, which are no more than opinion pieces of many leaders in the Body of Christ, I often find myself saying the same type of statement, "I don't think that this brother has yet to meet the Holy Spirit." Because, if there was an intimate knowledge of the person of the Holy Spirit *and* His operation, then they would not be teaching the saints of God to spurn, disbelieve, or be leery and suspicious of these things; nor of the teachers and proponents, nor of the brethren who operate in them. But, people being people, many Christians are more inclined to believe an institutional representative with the title of Doctor, Professor, or Pastor, without requiring the necessity of experiential, empirical knowledge that conforms to a biblical standard. In the coming years, with what God is about to do in the Church at large, those days are ending.

It would seem logical that those of the brethren from Pentecostal/Charismatic streams, who are the ones who are the biggest proponents of receiving and flowing in this gift, would be leading the way in thoroughly and biblically articulating the need, use, purpose, nuances, and benefits of this amazing gift. Today, unfortunately, there seems to be a lack thereof, as the erroneous teachings far outweigh the accurate ones. A faithful dissertation on *any* of the spiritual gifts should inspire us to "earnestly desire" (1 Cor. 12:31) that said gift. Because every "good and perfect gift comes from the Father of lights", who would not want *any* and *all* of those gifts, if possible? It is incomprehensible to me that anyone would feel otherwise toward anything that God would want to give them.

Additionally, I believe there has been a massive failure to adequately address the specific objections, fears, and misconceptions that a majority of believers have against receiving and operating in this gift. There are vast multitudes of "good" Christians with bad doctrinal beliefs that need to be reasoned with through Scripture, logic, real-life experience, and power, to get them to open themselves up to greater levels of communion with, and power of, the Holy Spirit.

I find that even some of those who have the gift of tongues and use it in its many facets do not thoroughly understand it themselves, let alone lead and equip others in its reception and use.

Typically, once a believer receives tongues through the baptism of the Holy Spirit, they are not further educated on it. The debriefing from this power encounter with God goes something like, "Okay, you've got it. Now, just do it all of the time, and trust that God is working through it!" It's funny how, because of the nature of tongues, this is good advice that does help tremendously. But it still does not lead to that person entering into a full understanding of what they have just received, nor to using it to its fullest purposes. Nor does it enable them to replicate it in and articulate it to other people.

It is into this void that I hope to launch this book.

I have written the chapters in question form so that even a casual glance at the Table of Contents might catch one's eye with a question to which they have been burning to know the answer.

I pray that reading this will kindle a burning desire to go after and receive this incredible gift from God. Or, if you already have it, to ignite you to train, equip, and empower others to use it more effectively and with greater faith and understanding.

For The King & His Kingdom!

Chapter Two

To Whose Voices Are You Listening? Opinions vs. Works

Whose Idea Was This Anyways?

In my church upbringing, I was never exposed to, or ever a member of, any Pentecostal or Charismatic church, movement, or doctrine. In fact, I was raised on the complete opposite end of the spectrum. I had no idea whatsoever about them other than, by word of mouth, that they were weird and bad, and that I should never have anything to do with them. It was a learned spiritual prejudice based on fear and ignorance. For most people, their fears of other different people groups are entirely based on ignorance of that particular people group, whether it be a different group based on race, religion, doctrine, political or social status, or any other differential. These fears impede honest, candid dialogue that would, at the very least, better facilitate more understanding between people; and at the very best, better facilitate unity.

The fact of the matter is that the idea of all Christians receiving the baptism of the Holy Spirit (BOTHS) and the ability to speak/pray in tongues IS NOT an idea that originated with Pentecostals and Charismatics. Whether you like it or not, both of those realities were instituted by God Almighty Himself. No human being would ever, in a million years, come up with something so "out there" or foreign to basic human wisdom and understanding. It is just too unnatural and foolish for our human reasoning.

There is a history of precious saints who were part of a multitude of various denominations and Christian movements, who loved the Lord and were hungry to experience His Kingdom that they were continuously reading about in the Word, but had never experienced for themselves. They were the ones who continued to seek the Lord as to why these things were not a reality for themselves when it was such an integral and powerful aspect of the early Church that is found in Scripture. They questioned, they sought, they found, they experienced it. They never started out trying to be a new movement, but they had received the same Pentecostal experience that the believers had in the book of Acts. Those saints who experienced this in 1901 were labeled "the Pentecostals". The truths that they rediscovered have forever changed Christianity back into a closer image of the first Church that Jesus left to us, and that the New Testament repeatedly speaks about. Since the first Church and throughout Church history, there have always been saints who have had those spiritual, biblical experiences, and were persecuted for it: the Ante-Nicene Church, the Monastics, the Montanists, the Cathari, the Waldenses, various Reformers, the Anabaptists, the

Quakers, the Moravians, the Methodists, and right up until the Pentecostals in 1901, and the Charismatics since the 1960's.[1]

I started the same way. I did not seek out Pentecostalism or Charismatic expressions, as I was cautioned against those who practiced them as a whole. I just wanted God. I needed more of Him, at whatever cost. I loved and taught the Word, as I came from a church movement that was known as, and prided itself on, knowing and teaching the Bible expositorily. But I wanted to do more to help people than just give them Bible verses to think about. I was hungry. But I was also honest enough to admit that I lacked the power to really help people with their very serious, real-life needs. God had directed my steps to a home fellowship where there were those who knew Him in profoundly more intimate and powerful ways than I could have possibly dreamed. And all it took was one evening of attendance, one time of me saying, "Yes!" to Him and His *fullness*, and I was forever changed, never to look back again.

So, if experiencing that which the one hundred-and-twenty disciples experienced in the upper room on the Day of Pentecost in Acts chapter 2 makes me a Pentecostal, then I guess I am, for I have had that Pentecostal experience as well. If believing that water baptism in the name of the Father, Son, and Holy Spirit is reserved only for those of an age where they are old enough to have made and understood a decision to trust in Jesus Christ and make Him the Lord of their life makes me a Baptist, then I guess I am that too. If believing that the local

---

1 Read *2000 years of Charismatic Christianity* by Dr. Eddie L. Hyatt, in order to consider that there has been a continuous string of supernatural graces (spiritual gifts) that have never vacated the Church since the Day of Pentecost in Acts 2.

church should have a group of elders/bishops leading and tending to the care of the people of that congregation makes me a Presbyterian/Episcopalian, then I guess I am accounted as such. If believing that salvation comes by grace, through faith alone in Jesus, makes me a Lutheran, then I am one of those as well. These beliefs are not denominational in nature; they are BIBLICAL.

Charismatic is the term that comes from the Greek word *charisma*, or *divinely conferred grace, gift, or power*. In the Bible, when Jesus and all of His followers healed sickness and disease, gave people prophetic words that were an answer to prayer or a key to their destiny, cast demons out of someone who was suffering in bondage, or laid hands on fellow believers and they were filled with the Holy Spirit and spoke with tongues—they were being charismatic—or operating in the grace and power that they had received from God, as was expected of them.

So, if I believe that I am commissioned by Jesus to do the same, and I go out and do that, does that make me a Charismatic? Well, if the works fit. No amount of money on earth would convince me to lay it all aside, for they are the works which my Lord commanded us to do before He left the earth. It is life to those who benefit from it. Not to mention, it is thoroughly biblical, *whatever* you want to label it. It is the same living water that Jesus dispensed. And let's be honest... not doing it is very, very, UNBIBLICAL.

> *Truly, truly, I say to you, he who believes in Me, the works that I do,* ***he will do also****; and greater works than these he will do; because I go to the Father.* John 14:12

Anyone who does not share this viewpoint must realize that your disagreement is not with Pentecostalism and Charismatics; it is with the Lord Himself. Sincerely inquire of Him as to why He picked such strange and difficult-to-accept ways to move upon Man (Hint: I answer this later in the book).

The "Caesar's Verdict" Trap

One thing that I do not understand is that if there is a *biblical precedent* for a spiritual experience/encounter that people are also experiencing today, why do so many Christians still deny or denounce that it is true or genuine? Usually, this is because we have come from a background that has taught against it, or we have had a negative experience with or heard negative comments about people who move in these things. But, most of the time, this cynicism stems from unbelief, offense, uncomfortability, or a simple lack of understanding.

When congregants have questions about these things because they have not experienced them for themselves, they inquire of their spiritual leader(s), which is appropriate. What has happened in our churches is that the congregation is looking to their leader for an answer regarding these things—what to believe—because they believe that the pastor will know better. Now, I am not equating church leaders to Caesar! But I am painting an analogy that allows you to envisage my point.

To me, it is reminiscent of the days of the Roman Coliseum, when once one gladiator subdued his opponent, he would look up to Caesar with sword raised, and await the final verdict—thumbs up, or thumbs down—life or death.

In the same way that the gladiators and Roman citizens of old would hold their breath in expectation of the final ruling, congregants await the assessment of their leader as to the veracity and validity of these spiritual topics, whether for or against. It is this specific leader's assessment that will accomplish one of four things in the people:

1. Protect from deception and false doctrine.
2. Expose to deception and false doctrine.
3. Propel God's people into discovering greater Kingdom truths and fulfillment.
4. Stunt and/or abort the spiritual growth of His people.

As leaders, just as Caesar's verdict was absolute and of a life-or-death magnitude, so is our responsibility and accountability of no less importance to a church's and an individual's spiritual life.

In ancient Rome, Caesar knew best because he was a god (and had an army). In our day, pastors/teachers are supposed to know best because they know God better (so we assume), and they typically know His Word the best. But is that supposition on our part weighty enough to warrant an all-out acceptance of their point of view? Or is there another common-sense litmus test?

"Those Who Can, Do. Those Who Can't, Teach."

This is a famous quote from George Bernard Shaw's 1903 play, *Man and Superman*. It is an adage that is memorable because so many times in life, it is true. The essence is that those who cannot do something well enough to make a living at it must resort to teaching others how to do it, where they will never be expected to replicate it or prove their proficiency in what they are teaching. Unfortunately, in the Church, this is all too common.

We expect our leaders or pastors to have all of the answers that we need. That is an unreasonable expectation at best and is the main reason why true biblical leadership consists of a plurality of leaders and varied graces (apostles, prophets, evangelists, pastors/teachers). When a church or fellowship has this unbiblical perspective and demand upon their pastor/teacher, it poses a two-fold problem:

1) The pastor, as the spiritual leader, feels pressure to have an answer for everyone on everything, and if he does not, then he must come up with one. Besides, it's his job, right? He's the leader. If he does not know, then what are the rest of us supposed to think? So rather than say, "I don't know. What do you think? Let's seek God together on this," the pastor feels compelled to be able to teach and explain the theology behind whatever it is, according to his understanding alone. That's a tough gig.

2) Since the pastor is the central authority in the respective church, and he probably has more biblical insight, knowledge, and experience than anyone else in the local assembly, what he says is usually gospel and the final word on any given topic. Some followers do not feel equipped enough to even question the respective conclusion or doctrine being taught. Or worse, some leaders are not secure enough in themselves to tolerate even being questioned. So, whatever the leader espouses, this becomes the viewpoint of all of the congregants and the respective church.

Is it any wonder why James said,

> *"Let not many of you become teachers, my brethren, knowing that as such* ***we will incur a stricter judgment****."* James 3:1

The fact is that there are many in the Body of Christ today who will believe a doctrine, theology, or viewpoint to be true based on the espouser's reputation, title or position, success and accomplishments, influence, size of church or ministry, or even the way of dress or personality of a pastor or leader. *None of these things* is a legitimate reason for believing the truth and validity of any proposed doctrine.

Get ready for this bomb… not even a person's character is reason enough to accept a doctrinal viewpoint. Even though character speaks to one's integrity and to the fact that they are not knowingly and willfully deceiving people, they still can be sincerely wrong. There is nothing in godly character, per se, that is an insurance policy against falling for deception. Yet, godly wisdom, patience, and prudence can prevent one from casting hasty disparagement or making premature judgments on any given subject. A great example of this character is the Pharisee, Gamaliel, in Acts 5:33-39:

> *When they heard this, they were furious and plotted to kill them* (Peter & John). *Then one in the council stood up, a Pharisee named Gamaliel, a teacher of the law held in respect by all the people, and commanded them to put the apostles outside for a little while. And he said to them: "Men of Israel,* ***take heed to yourselves what you intend to do regarding these men.*** *For some time ago Theudas rose up, claiming to be somebody. A number of men, about four hundred, joined him. He was slain, and all who obeyed him were scattered and came to nothing. After this man, Judas of Galilee rose up in the days of the census, and drew away many*

> *people after him. He also perished, and all who obeyed him were dispersed. And now I say to you, keep away from these men and let them alone;* ***for if this plan or this work is of men, it will come to nothing; but if it is of God, you cannot overthrow it—lest you even be found to fight against God.*** *"* Acts 5:33-39

The greatest thing that we can have to ensure doctrinal correctness is an openness to "the Spirit of Truth who leads and guides you into all truth," tethered to a *working knowledge* of the Word of God. Desiring to know the whole truth and nothing but the truth is a function of an individual's heart. If there is something in you that is willing to disregard certain facts or Scriptures because they do not line up with what you believe, have been taught, or are uncomfortable with, then you will be deceived to some extent. Conversely, if you have a heart that wants to know the truth regardless of what it will cost you, because you are finding that certain realities are in your life that are not lining up with what the Word of God says, then you will discover that truth. The Holy Spirit will see to it that you hit pay dirt, whatever it takes.

Teaching From Experience, Not Theory

One of the most common-sense and logical parameters that can be used to judge whether you should believe the validity of something that is being taught is this: is this person/leader/pastor proficient in actually *doing* the thing that they are teaching? I stand in amazement at what Christians will believe and defend tooth and nail simply because they heard it from some leader they respect, but who has never actually practiced the thing on which they are teaching.

We all would agree that if someone professes that they are a Christian but has no subsequent fruit in their life and no tell-tale signs that follow an authentic, regenerated disciple of Jesus Christ, then we should question that person's profession. In principle, this is no different.

Some all-too-common examples are:

- A leader who has never been used to heal anyone, teaching on healing.
- A leader who has never received the baptism of the Holy Spirit for himself, nor has laid hands on someone to receive it, teaching on it.
- A leader who has never cast out a demon teaches about deliverance and how Christians can't have a demon.
- A leader whose marriage is in shambles, teaching how to have a healthy marriage.
- A leader who is bound up in legalism, teaching grace, identity, and sonship.
- A leader who has never led anyone to the Lord, teaching how to evangelize.
- A leader who has never spoken in tongues, teaching on tongues.

The common thread that exists throughout most of the above examples is that they are all topics that are usually taught with a negative connotation or are said to be outright obsolete for today, when they are taught by people who do not operate in them as a regular outflow of their Christianity. This is similar to the sin of pride that has plagued religious leaders throughout history, and specifically, the Pharisees and Sadducees, whose premise of acceptance was, "Well, if *I'm* not experiencing it, then it's probably not God."

Conversely, this is not to say that you cannot teach something unless you are proficient in it. Many times, for myself, if I am not knowledgeable or proficient in an area of the Kingdom, I will put myself in a position where I have to teach it so that I force myself to grow in my knowledge of it. But when I do teach it, I do not portray an air of authority for the people to see as if I am an expert on the topic, and I have years of experience to authenticate my opinions of what I'm teaching. I leave it open to the possibility that I may be wrong. Nor do I recklessly and thoughtlessly condemn others in the Body who have not come to the same conclusions to which I have come. That is hypocrisy and is dangerous to portray to a group of growing believers who have yet to form a doctrinal opinion about the subject in question and are readily apt to adopt every word that I teach as gospel truth because I am their leader. This can be scary.

In our regular, everyday lives, we easily see the wisdom in prescribing this commonsense approach of listening to people who actually do the things that they teach. When we want to start a business, we seek the counsel of a successful businessperson. When we need new brakes put on our vehicle, we take it to a mechanic who has done many brakes. We do not take it to a used car salesman or to a place that only does oil changes and smog checks. They may all know all about cars, but do they know brakes specifically? We would never entrust the well-being of our precious families to someone who has never changed brakes before but has only read about how to do it in a *Popular Mechanics* magazine article or a *Chilton's Guide*.

Similarly, let's say that you have to have a life-saving surgery, and the choice before you is this: a young surgeon who is fresh out of one of the most prestigious medical schools in the country, where he graduated with the title of Valedictorian, Magna Cum Laude, at the top of his class. Though he has never performed surgery before, you will be his first. Or secondly, you have a surgeon who graduated from a middle-of-the-road, obscure medical school with about a C grade average, ten years ago. But, for the last 10 years, he has performed hundreds of successful operations of the same kind that you will need and has gained a solid reputation because of it. Into whose hands would you prefer to put your life? The one with the book knowledge but no experience, or the one with the book knowledge and the experience of doing what the book says regularly, but may not be so scholarly?

Sadly, the predominant voices that are being heeded in the Church today are those that have a title, respect, and Book knowledge. But they themselves cannot manifest its works.... which biblically speaking, "makes the Word of no effect." They are also quick to authoritatively condemn and cast aspersions on those who do produce these works of the Spirit, to obscure the fact that they do not.

So please understand that this book, along with all my teachings, is written from this perspective. If I am teaching it, I am also doing or have done it, as a matter of course. This is not theory, as these are teachings from first-hand experience that align with the spirit and heart of Scripture. Why would you listen to me or anyone else otherwise? You would not if you used wisdom and common sense. Jesus said,

> *"If I* ***<u>do not do</u>*** ***the works*** *of My Father,* ***do not believe*** *Me; but if* ***I <u>do</u>****, though you do not believe Me,* ***<u>believe the works</u>****, that you may know and believe that the Father is in Me, and I in Him."* John 10:37-38

Experience *does* matter. Prophetically speaking, I will tell you that the days of leaders in the Church only having good or right-sounding teaching or words, without the accompanying works or demonstration of that truth, are going to be confronted by the Lord Himself as He is in our midst.

> *For the kingdom of God is* ***not in <u>word</u> but in <u>power</u>****.* 1 Corinthians 4:20

> *And my speech and my preaching were not with* ***persuasive <u>words</u> of human wisdom****, but* ***<u>in demonstration</u> of the Spirit and of power****...* 1 Corinthians 2:4

> *But I will come to you shortly, if the Lord wills, and I will know,* ***<u>not the word</u> of those who are puffed up, <u>but the power</u>.*** 1 Corinthians 4:19

Even if you have apprehensions about the gift of tongues, please, at least be open to those who actually do "the works" in question. You have nothing to lose and more of Him and His Kingdom to gain!

> *"The Son of Man came eating and drinking, and you say, 'Here is a glutton and a drunkard, a friend of tax collectors and sinners.'* ***But wisdom is proved right by all her children*** *(the works)."* Luke 7:34-35 *NIV (parentheses added)*

Chapter Three

"Didn't Paul Warn Us in 1 Corinthians 14 Against Tongues?"

FOR EASE OF REFERENCE

1 Corinthians 14 (NKJV)

Prophecy and Tongues

14 *Pursue love, and desire spiritual gifts, but especially
that you may prophesy. 2 For he who speaks in a
tongue does not speak to men but to God, for no one
understands him; however, in the spirit he speaks mysteries.
3 But he who prophesies speaks edification and exhortation and
comfort to men. 4 He who speaks in a tongue edifies himself, but
he who prophesies edifies the church. 5 I wish you all spoke with
tongues, but even more that you prophesied; for he who
prophesies is greater than he who speaks with tongues, unless
indeed he interprets, that the church may receive edification.*

Tongues Must Be Interpreted

*6 But now, brethren, if I come to you speaking with tongues,
what shall I profit you unless I speak to you either by revelation,*

by knowledge, by prophesying, or by teaching? [7] Even things
without life, whether flute or harp, when they make a sound,
unless they make a distinction in the sounds, how will it be
known what is piped or played? [8] For if the trumpet makes an
uncertain sound, who will prepare for battle? [9] So likewise you,
unless you utter by the tongue words easy to understand, how
will it be known what is spoken? For you will be speaking into
the air. [10] There are, it may be, so many kinds of languages in
the world, and none of them is without significance.
[11] Therefore, if I do not know the meaning of the language, I
shall be a foreigner to him who speaks, and he who speaks will
be a foreigner to me. [12] Even so you, since you are zealous for
spiritual gifts, let it be for the edification of the church that you
seek to excel.

[13] Therefore let him who speaks in a tongue pray that he may
interpret. [14] For if I pray in a tongue, my spirit prays, but my
understanding is unfruitful. [15] What is the conclusion then? I
will pray with the spirit, and I will also pray with the
understanding. I will sing with the spirit, and I will also sing
with the understanding. [16] Otherwise, if you bless with the spirit,
how will he who occupies the place of the uninformed say
"Amen" at your giving of thanks, since he does not understand
what you say? [17] For you indeed give thanks well, but the other
is not edified.

[18] I thank my God I speak with tongues more than you all; [19] yet
in the church I would rather speak five words with my
understanding, that I may teach others also, than ten thousand
words in a tongue.

Tongues as a Sign to Unbelievers

[20] Brethren, do not be children in understanding; however, in
malice be babes, but in understanding be mature.

[21] In the law it is written:

> *"With men of other tongues and other lips*
> *I will speak to this people;And yet, for all that, they*
> *will not hear Me," says the Lord.*

22 Therefore tongues are for a sign, not to those who believe but to unbelievers; but prophesying is not for unbelievers but for those who believe. 23 Therefore if the whole church comes together in one place, and all speak with tongues, and there come in those who are uninformed or unbelievers, will they not say that you are out of your mind? 24 But if all prophesy, and an unbeliever or an uninformed person comes in, he is convinced by all, he is convicted by all. 25 And thus the secrets of his heart are revealed; and so, falling down on his face, he will worship God and report that God is truly among you.

Order in Church Meetings

26 How is it then, brethren? Whenever you come together, each of you has a psalm, has a teaching, has a tongue, has a revelation, has an interpretation. Let all things be done for edification. 27 If anyone speaks in a tongue, let there be two or at the most three, each in turn, and let one interpret. 28 But if there is no interpreter, let him keep silent in church, and let him speak to himself and to God. 29 Let two or three prophets speak, and let the others judge. 30 But if anything is revealed to another who sits by, let the first keep silent. 31 For you can all prophesy one by one, that all may learn and all may be encouraged. 32 And the spirits of the prophets are subject to the prophets. 33 For God is not the author of confusion but of peace, as in all the churches of the saints.

34 Let your women keep silent in the churches, for they are not permitted to speak; but they are to be submissive, as the law also says. 35 And if they want to learn something, let them ask their own husbands at home; for it is shameful for women to speak in church.

36 Or did the word of God come originally from you? Or was it you only that it reached? 37 If anyone thinks himself to be a prophet or spiritual, let him acknowledge that the things which I write to you are the commandments of the Lord. 38 But if anyone is ignorant, let him be ignorant.

39 Therefore, brethren, desire earnestly to prophesy, and do not forbid to speak with tongues. 40 Let all things be done decently and in order.

An Honest Look at What Paul's Point Was to the Corinthians

"Didn't Paul warn us in 1 Corinthians *against* tongues?" Well, to answer simply… No, not at all. In fact, there is much more positive that Paul mentions about the gift of tongues than there is negative. Yet, because it is framed within Paul's corrective adjustment of its use within a public church service, it comes across with a negative connotation. If you read Chapter 14 objectively through an unbiased filter, as if you are reading it for the first time, you will see. Let us look at these in detail.

We know that in any event, it is the negative that seems to get more attention than the positive. Our news broadcasts are built upon this fact. When I was the manager of a corporate-owned coffeehouse, there was a principle taught that said a customer will not tell others about the ten great customer experiences they had, but they will tell several people about the one negative experience that they had. This is just the truth of our human nature, and when you look at First Corinthians honestly, specifically looking at it with this in mind, I believe that you will be astonished by the results.

Remember that First Corinthians is simply a letter that Paul wrote to the believers in Corinth. He preached the Gospel in Corinth, converted many, filled them with the Holy Spirit, and taught them the basics of a life following Jesus Christ. These believers fellowshipped together regularly to learn more about this new way of living as well as to share and encourage each other in what God was doing in their midst. As they congregated together, they became a "congregation". We forget that the early Church did not "do church" the way that we do today. We have adopted a very business-like, organizational structure to the church today, where order and leadership hierarchy are established before much of anything else. When people come into this set order and way of doing things today, they are expected to conform and comply with the system, or they will be ushered out as non-compliant distractors. The early churches were still trying to figure this whole thing out. They would meet in all sorts of different venues: public squares, homes, fields, over meals, etc. They would worship and talk about God and what the Scriptures said. They would exercise their newfound spiritual gifts on each other and those outside of the Church in the marketplace.

You can imagine that there was consistently a multitude of questions from everyone, which we take for granted today. These were not structured "services" that we are used to going to today. The first Christians, even the Disciples, were all "in process". The difficulties and potential discomforts and conflicts that can arise from a free-flowing meeting are some of the reasons why the Holy Roman Catholic Church established the Mass, taking the worship service out of the people's hands and putting it into the hands of the "professionals"—the priests. Thus, liturgy was born.

Paul, on hearing about some of the occurrences that were happening in Corinth, wrote this letter to help straighten out some of these problem areas. He addressed: 1) divisions arising among the brethren around which particular Christian teachers people were following 2) people not doing their part or honoring other's different roles within the church 3) immorality, carnality, and immaturity being tolerated 4) many questions regarding Christians in marriage and celibacy 5) eating food sacrificed to idols 6) his critics and his right to provision from the church 7) the taking of communion and specifics to conducting the times of worship when the saints would congregate.

1 Corinthians 14 is where Paul addresses the issues of speaking in tongues, only relating to its use in a church worship meeting, in particular. To better understand this chapter, we must try and identify where the new believers were in their understanding of these new spiritual experiences. More than likely, this new movement of "The Way", as it was known, took the Corinthians by storm. If you were a Corinthian, one day you were just living your life, and the next thing you know, you were hearing amazing stories of miracles, healings, demons being cast out of people, and of the resurrection from the dead of a Jewish guy named Jesus. You also would have heard that everyone who believes in this Jewish Messiah: Jew and Gentile, male and female, rich and poor, master and servant, young and old alike, has an experience where God Himself comes into them and you experience this new life and power. All the participants in this new faith are having radical spiritual encounters and major heart and life changes that sound like fiction when measured by normal standards.

You would have gone to witness this stirring of "strange things" for yourself. If you responded, you would have had hands laid on you by the preachers of this message, and you would have then experienced firsthand knowledge of this new life and been thoroughly convinced. At this time, there was no book of instruction or set parameters of conduct by which to judge, understand, or regulate these things. Everyone involved was trying to get a handle on exactly what it all meant as some astonishing revelations and discoveries seemed to be happening daily. The leaders and preachers of this faith would continually tell you of the Jewish Holy Scriptures (the Old Testament only) and how this was all a manifestation of the promises that God had made to the children of Abraham, but were now available to everyone and anyone who would believe. The more you were open to and had the childlike faith to believe… the more you received.

When believers "received the Holy Spirit" through the laying on of hands, many would begin shouting praises in a language that they did not know, many would weep, laugh, yell, fall, shake, etc., which was mistaken for drunkenness (Acts 2). Some would do all the above. The reactions to the infilling of the God of the universe and His power into human vessels would be as varied as there are needs and personalities of people. But one thing was universal: you would have a heightened awareness of the presence of God with spiritual eyes and ears that enabled you to have a greater spiritual sensitivity, as well as receive accompanying spiritual powers, or gifts, to use to glorify God in this new life of faith.

When the masses of new believers would come together in whatever manner or respective venue, they would use or practice these new gifts. They would share what was happening to each other regarding these gifts and the experiences that they were having. Can you imagine the stories and testimonies that were rolling in daily? It must have seemed like a cross between a tidal wave and a three-ring circus… "multitudes being added daily". Oh, that we would see days like this again, where you are just hanging onto the ride for dear life. Go, God! Go!

If you have had the privilege of experiencing a powerful, supernatural move of God's Spirit, you can identify with this feeling and atmosphere where you are just trying to stay on your surfboard while riding the wave of God's Presence. If not, you will see Paul's letter through the lenses of a post-modern, pre-programmed, highly structured and organized, teaching-focused, church service attendee. Not even a participant. This lack of experiencing a living, vibrant, fluid, supernatural, member-participatory environment would lead you to some less-than-accurate conclusions about the details of what Paul is saying in 1 Corinthians 14. This is not prideful; it is just true, and those of you who have experienced an outpouring of God's Spirit know it.

As the tide of revival subsides, which it has always done, we then settle into times of cementing an understanding of and putting into practice the things that we have learned or experienced in revival. In His wisdom and graciousness, the Lord allows us time to digest everything that happened and hammer out a working theology of what we just experienced. When you think about it, that is really what all the New Testament epistles are—letters from trusted church leaders setting theology and parameters to the countless discoveries and revelations that were obtained through the last move of God in that city. Teaching and understanding are most definitely needed, but never as a complete substitute for the presence and the life of God being manifested in our midst. Biblically speaking, teaching is to always be a complement and companion to the works and manifestations of Christ. Teaching should lead us into more wisely using and more deeply receiving everything we can out of life in the Spirit.

In the Bible, in both Jesus' ministry and the early Church, teaching was *never* a stand-alone endeavor. For the Pharisees and Sadducees, it was. In much of Christendom today, it is as well. The quest for a proper and perfect doctrine, while not expecting a manifestation of that doctrine by the Spirit, is not a true replication of biblical, Kingdom living.

Most Christians' cursory knowledge of what the Bible says about tongues is negative, and usually by third-party hearsay. But when you unbiasedly read 1 Corinthians 14 within the context of what I have outlined, as well as Paul's very clear verbiage, you can only arrive at one conclusion:

There is **ONLY ONE** caveat about tongues that Paul writes about, and this one caveat is **NOT** negative. It is simply a directive that explains that this gift is ***not effective*** in one particular circumstance—***in speaking for public consumption within the church service,*** **WITHOUT** an interpreter. Paul says that **IT IS APPROPRIATE** to speak in tongues ***publicly*** in a church service **IF** there is someone with the gift of interpretation present, **OR** ***privately*** for one's self-edification in worship and prayer. And we are **NOT** to forbid it.

Any other conclusion drawn is a prejudiced and willful disregard of what is plainly written and meant, and falls completely outside of the context in which it is written. To teach otherwise is irresponsible and not supported by Scripture anywhere.

The following is a diagram that outlines the specific uses and appropriate applications for speaking in tongues in its various operations. I will discuss this in further detail in Chapter 5, Section IV – *Understanding the Different Kinds of Tongues*. Notice the differentiation between "private" and "public" use.

This is *the* key to appropriately understanding the context in which Paul is writing 1 Corinthians 14.

SPECIFIC USES OF SPEAKING IN TONGUES

Forum:	*Private* Use		*Public* Ministry	
	↙	↘	↙	↘
Manifestation of Tongues:	**Personal Prayer/ Praise Language**	**Intercession**	**Sign & Wonder**	**Prophetic Word**
Initiator:	Self	Holy Spirit	Holy Spirit	Holy Spirit
Strengthens:	Self	Self/Others (Depending on for whom you're interceding)	Others - Unbelievers (Hearers experiencing the miraculous; under-standing the message without interpretation)	Others - Believers (Upon hearing the interpretation)
Scriptural Refs.:	1 Cor. 13:1 1 Cor. 14:2,4,14-17 Acts 2:1-12 Acts 10:44-46 Acts 19:1-7 Ephesians 6:18 Jude 1:20	1 Cor. 13:1 1 Cor. 14:2, 14-15 Romans 8:26-27	1 Cor. 13:1 1 Cor. 14:21-22 Acts 2:1-12	1 Cor. 13:1 1 Cor. 14:4-6, 13, 26-27

"He Who Prophesies is Greater Than He Who Speaks with Tongues"

I have heard this statement in verse 5 used by teachers as additional negative fodder to heap upon the use of tongues as a lesser ministry, so why should we even want it?

Remember, Paul is specifically addressing the fact that when you are speaking publicly to people, they must be able to understand what you are saying. And with tongues, people do not, unless there is an interpreter. So, regarding a publicly practiced gift in a church service, a tongue *without* interpretation is not beneficial to the other congregants because nobody understands the speaker (verse 2). It in no way connotes that the gift itself, nor the person who practices it, is lesser than the gift or the person who prophesies. It is simply saying that *for public speaking in a church service,* it is less desirable than prophesying, *for only the fact that prophesying is in an understandable language, and tongues is not*. This viewpoint is further proven by the very next sentence in the verse:

> *I wish you all spoke with tongues, but even more that you prophesied; for he who prophesies is greater than he who speaks with tongues,* ***unless indeed he interprets,*** *that the church may receive edification.* 1 Corinthians 14:5

The words, "unless indeed he interprets, that the church may receive edification", specifically show that the ONLY reason why one is "greater" or to say more accurately, "more desirable or effective" in a church service is based upon the sole fact of relating the information in a known spoken language of the hearers. This is common sense. The reading of verses 6 through 25 will further prove that Paul's sole concern about tongues is that nobody can hope to understand what is being said without an interpreter, as it makes no sense, so it is pointless to publicly make a statement in tongues to the congregation without an interpreter.

Simply put, you do not drive in a screw with a hammer. You can, but it's ugly. A screwdriver is a more effective tool to drive in a screw, but you do not throw your hammer away because you have a screwdriver. Regarding screws, one who has a screwdriver is "greater" than one who has a hammer. Inversely, driving and pulling nails with a screwdriver is equally ineffective; thus, you need the hammer. As you will see in subsequent chapters, tongues are a "greater" gift than prophecy regarding many aspects of personal spiritual growth, as it can accomplish things that prophecy cannot.

This clarity of understanding Paul's intent and instructions is further evidenced by the many times that he repeatedly reiterates his positive outlook on the gift of tongues:

- *"He who speaks in a tongue edifies himself..."* v. 4
- *"I wish you all spoke with tongues..."* v. 5
- *"For you indeed give thanks well..."* v. 17
- *"I thank my God I speak with tongues more than you all..."* v. 18
- *"...**and do not forbid to speak with tongues.**"* v. 3

Any church doctrine or practice that forbids speaking in tongues is very clearly unbiblical.

Regulating Two Spiritual Gifts Out of the Church

Typically, there are three viewpoints that church

leaders take regarding speaking in tongues. First, there is the *cessationist* view, which says that tongues and all the supernatural gifts of the Spirit ceased with the passing of the first Apostles, or that they ceased upon the canonization (official completion and compilation) of Scripture.

Secondly, there is the viewpoint (to which I subscribe) that all the gifts are valid and in use today, that nothing has changed from the time of the birth of the Church at Pentecost, and that we should equip all the saints to function appropriately in their respective spiritual gifts in all situations.

The third, and most held viewpoint, is that there is an agreement doctrinally that tongues and spiritual gifts are for today, but the reality of fostering and experiencing these gifts either individually or corporately is very rare, and should not, or is not, necessarily to be pursued. From a self-preservation standpoint, this is the safest viewpoint for leaders to take, which does not truly serve the people but protects their own self-interests by avoiding offense, confusion, uncomfortability, or potential doctrinal disputes. The avoidance of these issues does not force the people of God to mature or grow in their understanding of the Lord, His Spirit, and His ways. It is the epitome of sacrificing long-term gain to avoid short-term pain.

Leaders who subscribe to this view realize that adhering to a cessationist viewpoint means that they would have to disregard much of New Testament doctrine, as well as the many reports of believers, and even possibly themselves, operating in spiritual gifts. The abundance of evidence of spiritual gifts being in operation today is just too prevalent to warrant outright cessationism.

Also, the verse, "and do not forbid to speak with tongues", is so plain that it would be a stretch in any interpretation to explain that directive away. But there is one way that leaders can limit, if not completely eradicate, the use of tongues within a fellowship while still verbally saying that they agree with tongues as a doctrine. And it is done in most Western churches today, whether inadvertently or purposefully.

In an effort to "protect the sheep" and stay doctrinally "pure", most church leaders have focused on Paul's teaching on tongues with a negative connotation, emphasizing the requirement of interpretation as the only legitimate and necessary means for tongues. Therefore, we focus on training people in the use of their spiritual gift of interpretation of tongues, through teaching, personal discipleship, and practice in corporate gatherings.... oh wait... **no, we don't!** We ***never*** talk about the gift of interpretation of tongues. We ***never*** teach it specifically, how it operates, or how to recognize it in you if it is operating, and how to do it correctly. In fact, the ***only*** discussion that we ever have about it is in the context of teaching that you are forbidden to speak in tongues in a public service without it, or when a congregant is getting reprimanded for speaking in tongues in a church service, and nobody steps up to interpret it.

Even most Spirit-filled people, who may have the gift, are not aware of it because they have never had the opportunity to be put into a position where they could use it. This circular reasoning, rooted in "protectionism", has caused the near extinction of the gift of interpretation of tongues in the Church. It is not that God has stopped giving it, but it is the fact that most people who are ordained to have it remain unaware of it because of the climate that we have instituted in our public church services.

The reasoning goes something like this: to be biblical, the "rules of the house" (in no uncertain terms) are that no one may speak in tongues in a public gathering unless there is another person with the gift of interpretation present. But because we do not help discover, nurture, or encourage the gift, we do not know who may have it. And, since we are not aware of anyone with the gift, out of fear of being rebellious, we do not speak in tongues in a service… ***ever***. So, because we *never* give a prophetic utterance through the gift of tongues publicly in a service, people who may have the gift of interpretation are *never* exposed to it. Thus, they will *never* have any idea that they can pursue and develop it. So, everyone is *ever* ignorant of the supernatural possibilities that we forego every service. That's a lot of "never, ever's"!

Subsequently, most Western churches remain uninformed and inexperienced in both speaking in tongues and the interpretation of tongues, and all their benefits. This ought not to be so. All the promises of God *should be* "Yes!" and "Amen!", and none of them should remain covered by a blanket of leeriness and fear.

And let's be totally honest, most pastors do not want this to happen in a public service because it is like walking on a high wire above the crowd. You must deal with offended and uninformed people; you must exercise faith in the Holy Spirit to show up; faith in your fellow brethren to be obedient; faith in your fellow brethren to be accurate; and if necessary, publicly correct something if it is wrong. Most pastors do not think that all the possible downsides outweigh the upside of whatever the prophetic word may be. This is the state of the modern church service. We value propriety, predictability, and unprovocativeness over a spontaneous flow of the Holy Spirit through His people. It is much easier just to have musical worship, announcements, a teaching, then an altar call, with no hiccups and moments of uncomfortability. While this may be convenient, it does not train Christians how to manifest, nor to correctly discern, the Kingdom of God in all its variations within the church service. This also keeps the majority of congregants in perpetual infancy and "spectator mode" regarding the spirit realm.

> ***Do not quench the Spirit. Do not despise prophecies****. Test all things; hold fast what is good...*
> 1 Thessalonians 5:19-21

Thus, by regulation, negative teaching, and subsequent fear of infringing these rules, these two gifts have become scarce in the Western Church service, especially the interpretation of tongues.

> *He (Jesus) was also saying to them, "You are experts at setting aside and nullifying the commandment of God in order to keep your [man-made] tradition and regulations."* Mark 7:9 *AMP*

A Public Tongue Given as Prophecy

I just wanted to give a brief word about exercising a tongue as a prophetic gift, as many people who have not done it believe that it is the same as tongues as a prayer language.

In the same way that I can speak in English but can only prophesy in English if the Lord is directing me to or because I have a prophetic gift and I am seeing something in the spirit realm; I can pray in tongues, but it only becomes a prophetic tongue, if the Lord is providing the unction or grace for it to be a prophetic word. Having the first ability does not presume having the second.

When I have given a prophetic tongue to a congregation, I believe that it was an outflow of my prophetic gifting, operating as a tongue. While I was in a church service, I was praying in tongues privately under my breath as I often do, to better align my senses with what the Holy Spirit was doing in the meeting. I noticed that I began praying the same phrase repeatedly without variation. With this realization, I wondered if this was a prophetic tongue for the entire congregation—a prophetic word. I sensed in my spirit that it was. It was no different than if I were sensing in my spirit that I had a prophetic word for the congregation in English.

Because I was in a Spirit-filled church where spiritual gifts were not just tolerated but encouraged, I knew that I could give the tongue and then wait to see if anyone had the interpretation. I was not aware of any specific person present with the gift of interpretation because, in today's church atmosphere, it is rare that a person would even know it. But I knew that the pastors' hearts were to go with whatever the Holy Spirit wanted to do and that we would work through it all, regardless. They did not want to miss a thing that the Lord was possibly doing.

There must be grace and encouragement given to the people of God so that they may feel confident to proverbially "step out of the boat and onto the water" in the spirit, with these things. It can be quite challenging to overcome the fear of not getting it right in a public setting, thus, resigning ourselves to remaining seated in silence.

Fortunately, after I spoke the tongue out loud to the congregation (the same phrase repeated itself three times over), someone then interpreted it into English as a prophetic word from which the entire congregation could receive edification. Both the interpreter and I had stepped out in faith, and the Lord had met us "out on the water", where we all supernaturally experienced His Kingdom.

As you will come to better understand after reading this book, when I stood up to speak the prophetic tongue, I did not have any idea what was going to come out of my mouth! I followed the leading of the Holy Spirit, and it was His words that came out of my spirit, via my mouth. It was not my words coming out of my mind, via my mouth. I was completely stepping out in faith that what I was previously speaking privately was going to be repeated publicly when I did it. The Lord had used my prayer language to lead me into manifesting a prophetic tongue, which was an outflow of my prophetic gifting.

Chapter Four

"My Walk is Fine. Why Do I Need to Speak in Tongues?"

No Thanks, Lord—I'm Good

When I was in elementary school, I just wanted to do the minimum schoolwork that was required. I remember that when teachers made available additional assignments that were deemed "extra credit", I wanted no part of it unless, of course, my semester grade was suffering, for which I would get into trouble with my dad. Then, it was to save my own butt… literally. I never did any additional assignments for the joy and love of learning. But some did.

In fourth grade, there were girls like Jill Charney and Heather Compton—pretty, little girls whose desks were always clean and organized, who turned in all assignments on time with perfect penmanship, and who always did extra credit while I struggled to just finish the requirements. Their papers would come back with minimal red ink on it, save for a big smiley face and a "100% Great Job!" on top, and even sometimes accompanied by a gold star or a cool sticker. Irritating.

Of course, classmates like this throughout our school careers earned the moniker, "Teacher's Pet". Why? Because we saw the genuine pleasure and praise that they engendered in and from our teachers, and we wished that we could do it as well. What we were too young to understand, though, was that most teachers were there because they cared. They had a love for learning, and they wanted children to learn and to do the best of their ability. When students turned in good work, it shouted, "He/She's getting it!" It helped teachers to confirm within themselves that they were seeing the fulfillment of the supreme reason for choosing the teaching profession.

Similarly, when we in childlikeness, have an attitude of utter desperation to experience and know more of God, in whatever manner of way possible, we give that same pleasure to the Lord. If God has a single drop of something more of Himself and His Kingdom that He wants to give to me, then get out of my way, I'm coming after it! It is not that I *have to* speak in tongues; it is a privilege that I *get to* speak in tongues. Any other stance shows a problem at your core heart level. Why would anyone balk at *anything* that is given by the Lord?

"Why do I need to pray in tongues?" That is like saying, "Well, I'm alive, so why do I need to eat fruits and vegetables and exercise regularly?" The problem lies in the question itself. It is already coming from a faulty viewpoint of "Is it a requirement?" instead of "What an honor!" If it is not required by God and I do not see the benefit of it, then why do it?

When we portray by our actions or say in our hearts, "No thanks, Lord. I'm good. I don't think that's really necessary for me." It shows an unteachable spirit rooted in pride, where we think that we know what we need better than our Father does. Cutting yourself off from *anything* more that He has for you gives Him no pleasure and does not fulfill the supreme reason why He sent His Son to the Cross—to be one with you, sharing all.

The Miraculous Benefits of "Vitamin T"

I was raised in the Church. I have been in services and meetings in almost every venue imaginable and with people across the entire spectrum of Christianity. Not that I am trying to be crass or cheeky, but one thing I know to be true, in the majority of churches, when you say the "T" word (tongues), the reaction is just like if you had said the "F" word. That is how volatile, fearful, hostile, and misconstrued the assault is on the gift of tongues.

All of us, while watching television at one time or another, have seen an infomercial. An infomercial is an in-depth and extended commercial that attempts to demonstrate all the benefits of, and our need for, having a particular product, as well as testimonials from users of said product. One of the biggest industries that most effectively uses infomercials is Health and Wellness—exercise equipment, workouts, diets, and supplements. The most popular products seem to be those that promise the maximum number of results with the minimum amount of effort.

So, if you would indulge me for a moment, I am going to tell you about a "product" that can have a significant effect on your spiritual growth and health. If I could just tell you of the many benefits, biblically speaking, without telling you that it is tongues (thus avoiding your fears, prejudice, and preconceived notions), I believe that you would be among the first one-hundred callers dialing that 800 number on your screen for a bottle of "Vitamin T". Fortunately for you… It's free—shipping and handling included. The Operator is standing by.

From 1 Corinthians 14… A daily dose of Vitamin T gives you the following:

- Supernatural ability to speak to God, spirit to Spirit. (v. 2)
- The ability to pray out the unknown mysteries of God, directed by the Holy Spirit Himself. (v.2)
- The ability to build up, strengthen, and edify oneself spiritually at any time. (v.4)
- Be used as a vessel to bring forth a prophetic word from the Lord (v. 5)
- The ability to bypass our limited human knowledge and understanding to be able to pray God's perfect will, even when we do not know what it is. (v. 14)
- Can be exercised according to our own will, at our discretion, when needed. (v.15)
- Can be used compatibly with music and song. (v.15)
- The ability to give thanks well, directly from your spirit, even when you cannot articulate and put into words what you are feeling. (v.15-17)
- The opportunity to be a miraculous sign to unbelievers when you speak or are interpreted as, a known human language that you do not know or comprehend. (v.22)

So, putting all of the negative perceptions about tongues aside, if I was able to bottle these abilities with these promises and benefits, do you think most Christians would be interested in buying it? Who wouldn't?

After years of ministering to the Body, I know that people in their walks are set upon by problems, inabilities, and just being stuck. This spiritual "product" is a tool for, and solution to, many of those problems. Unfortunately, most believers cannot get past the offense of the packaging to partake of the wonders, promises, and spiritual health benefits of what is in the bottle and available to themselves—a sad and unnecessary reality.

> *...as His divine power has given to us all things that pertain to life and godliness...* 2 Peter 1:3

When most people read 1 Corinthians 14, they fail to notice all of the positive attributes of tongues that Paul mentions because it is shrouded in the one fact that Paul is teaching people that tongues are not the best spiritual tool or gift to be exercised publicly in a church meeting unless someone with the gift of interpretation is present. He finishes the entire instruction by admonishing that even though he is bringing guidance and correction to the use of tongues in a public service, we are "NOT TO FORBID TO SPEAK WITH TONGUES" in it (v. 39). Any other church practice or conclusion is a willful disregard of verse 39, and thus Holy Scripture.

Read the chapter again, now being mindful of the many benefits that he mentions. An analogy for this whole chapter is like telling a woman that she is wearing too much makeup. Makeup, when applied correctly, is meant to and does help to accentuate beauty. But when the amount of makeup used is over-the-top or applied incorrectly, it detracts from the woman's natural beauty, and she actually subverts the beauty that she is trying to achieve in the first place. This is Paul's point regarding tongues. He is not trying to abolish it. In fact, he endorses it, when done correctly.

Repenting, or changing your mind, about any negativity regarding tongues is the first step to receiving it and benefiting more from it if you have it already. Now let's look in greater detail at some of the above-mentioned beneficial claims:

The supernatural ability to speak to God, spirit to Spirit (v. 2)

> *For he who speaks in a tongue <u>does not speak to men but to God</u>...* (v. 2)

> *O my God, my soul is cast down within me; Therefore I will remember You ... <u>Deep calls unto deep</u> at the noise of Your waterfalls...* Psalm 42:6-7

Anyone who truly loves the Lord would be open to *any* method that enhances the level of intimacy and expression of our love and gratitude towards Him. Tongues provide that expression from the depths of our spirit, beyond human-directed words, that few other things can rival. It is truly miraculous and fulfilling.

Tongues are a spirit, or heavenly, language. It is a supernatural ability that God gives to His children upon receiving the baptism of the Holy Spirit (BOTHS), whereby they can commune with Him on an entirely different, spiritual level. Paul confirms this in 1 Corinthians 13:1, which is below.

1 Corinthians chapter 12 through 14 is Paul's entire dissertation on spiritual gifts, callings, motivational gifts, and proper use of them. The first verse of chapter 13, states, "Though I speak with the *tongues of men and of angels* but have

not love…" (v.1). When speaking in tongues, there can be two manifestations of it. The first is the "tongues of men", which I will detail in the latter part of this list. The second is the "tongues of angels". In chapter 13, Paul is referring to many of the spiritual gifts that we can have, but pointing out that regardless of what gifts we do have, if they are not motivated by love, then they are of no benefit to you, the worker of that gift. Motive and intention are of utmost importance in God's eyes. So, verse one states that there are two manifestations of tongues: 1) of men (known languages), and 2) of angels (unknown spirit language).

Regardless of whether you can receive this or are comfortable with this truth, it is an amazing biblical fact. Our Father gives us the ability to communicate spiritually on a whole other level, regardless of our intellect, education, Bible knowledge, or personal ability. It truly makes the deep things of the Kingdom available to *all*, and I find this truth simply astounding and of which I am so appreciative. In the Spirit, we all start from the same level playing field.

Another amazing truth of this spirit language that I have personally experienced myself can occur when we are asleep. When we sleep, what does our spirit do? When asleep, our mind, will, and emotions (our soul) dial down, but our spirit never sleeps. It does not need to. Our spirit is fully awake and receptive to the spirit realm. This is why God uses dreams so profusely throughout the Bible.

Many believers have had experiences where their spouse will hear them praying in tongues in their sleep or will wake themselves up to find that they are praying in tongues in their sleep. This is spirit-to-Spirit interaction with the Lord, which bypasses our minds and understanding.

Recently, I met a pastor who told me that years ago he had prayed in tongues once, briefly, while in a private devotion time in the woods. He was unfamiliar and uninformed about this gift due to his church background, and so never pursued it further. After we had talked for a couple of hours, and I had educated him on the nature and function of tongues (basically, the information in this book), a fire of excitement and hunger to encounter more of God was ignited in him. That very week, he called me to tell me that he had felt drawn to pray in tongues one night for a very long time while lying in bed, before going to sleep, and that it just flowed from within him like a river. Then, that night around 4 a.m., he awoke praying in tongues while in his sleep. Subsequently, he had received a powerful message to preach regarding a certain Scripture verse that was made alive to him. After he preached, he told me that during the sermon, he had never felt an anointing like that before while speaking.

Remember that giving us this ability was, and is, ENTIRELY God's idea. No man came up with it, so we would be wise to embrace it, discomfort, and all. The sooner that we do, the deeper we will be able to go in the Spirit.

The ability to pray out the mysteries of God, directed by the Holy Spirit Himself. (v.2)

The entirety of Chapter 6, *Why Do We Need Tongues When We Have the Bible?* (pg. 107), is dedicated to expounding upon this.

The ability to build up, strengthen, and edify oneself spiritually at any time. (v.4)

This essential benefit will be discussed in detail in Chapter 7, *Spirit Muscle*, under the section, "*Our God-given Spiritual Weight Set*" (pg. 155).

Be used as a vessel to bring forth a prophetic word from the Lord (v. 5)

> *I wish you all spoke with tongues, but even more that you prophesied; for he who prophesies is greater than he who speaks with tongues, unless indeed he interprets, that the church may receive edification.* (v. 5)

Another manifestation of the gift of tongues is its use to deliver prophecy. Just as someone who prophesies (speaks what God is currently saying) in a known language to the hearers, the person who feels led by the Holy Spirit to give a prophetic word to the hearers in an unknown tongue, would either need to interpret it themselves or wait for another person to give an interpretation after they give the word in tongues. So, in this way, someone who speaks in tongues can be used to give a prophetic word to the congregation, if feeling the unction of the Holy Spirit to do so.

In our current church service climate, it takes much courage, faith, and obedience to speak out in a tongue when you do not know what it means or what it will sound like. Also, you do not know if you or someone else will get an interpretation of it when you give it. Even if someone receives an interpretation from the Lord, they then must be courageous and obedient enough to step out and publicly say it. The only reason why you step out and do it at all is because you feel the insistence of the Holy Spirit, and you want everyone to be edified by what God is saying when it all comes together. I have witnessed this happening numerous times and have only been used one time in prophesying via tongues. When everyone steps out in faith, courage, and obedience, God always honors it, and it is always a blessing. It undoubtedly demonstrates our need for each other and each other's gifting in the Body of Christ.

I would again like to address the biggest reason that we rarely see this operate in most churches today. If a person with the spiritual gift of interpretation is required to give a public prophetic tongue, but we have a church culture that seriously frowns upon that manifestation of tongues, then how are people in the church supposed to even know if they have the gift of interpretation? If we have no interpreters, we never hear a prophetic tongue. if we never hear a prophetic tongue, then how do you know if you have an interpretation gift? So, we stay silent. It is a self-defeating cycle, keeping the Church in ignorance of this aspect of prophecy. And if the congregation in question does not even believe in or administer the baptism of the Holy Spirit (BOTHS), then none of this will ever happen anyway.

When my wife and I were newly married and she had just been filled with the Holy Spirit, we briefly attended a very small fellowship that believed and moved in all of the spiritual gifts. But regarding giving a prophetic tongue, the pastor, wanting to be sure that they followed Paul's instruction to the very letter, inadvertently quenched it from ever happening. He did this by creating an atmosphere and culture of, "You better be right, and that better be God!" When he gave instructions about how to do it "decently and in order," he rather harshly pointed a finger at the congregation and chided that if somebody gave a prophetic tongue, "there better be an interpretation!"

Well, as you can guess, there was never a prophetic tongue given in any of the services. My wife, who is extremely prophetic, and who was new to the spiritual gifts, recalls how scared his instruction made her, and that she was never going to give a tongue in a church service unless the heavens parted above her and an angel or Jesus Himself manifested to her and said, "Declarest thou the tongue which thou hath receiveth!" A perfect example of how we miss the forest for the trees to maintain "correctness."

How do you discover, practice, and grow in your spiritual gifts if you are expecting perfection from its inception? This kind of atmosphere and culture does nothing to foster stepping out in faith, taking risks for the Lord, and the benefit of learning from what works, as well as our mistakes. It shuts everything down for correctness' sake, sacrificing discovering, learning, and practical application, on the altar of an inert sense of "decent and in order". The purpose of a decent and orderly church service is to accommodate a stirring, life-giving expression of God's Spirit and His Word as it comes through His surrendered people. It is not the monolithic, end-all, sacrament that portrays a comatose propriety as God's ultimate goal for meeting together.

So, in the immortal words of Forrest Gump, "That's all I got to say, 'bout that". Not really, but that's another book…

The ability to bypass our limited human knowledge and understanding to be able to pray God's perfect will even when we do not know what it is! (v. 14)

This wonderful benefit will be covered extensively in Chapter 8, *How Can I Pray the Will of God When I Don't Know What It Is?* (pg. 169).

Can be exercised according to our own will, at our discretion, when needed. (v.15)

> *What is the conclusion then? I will pray with the spirit, and I will also pray with the understanding. I will sing with the spirit, and I will also sing with the understanding.* 1 Corinthians 14:15

Paul clearly states that we can both pray and sing in our known languages (the understanding), as well as our spiritual language/tongues (with the spirit). This shows that we are the ones exercising the gift of tongues by choice. We can choose to speak or sing, in our known language or with our spirit language.

There is a common misconception by those who have never spoken in tongues that one must wait until the Holy Spirit comes upon you and then He *makes* you speak in tongues when He wills it. This is untrue, as it is with most other spiritual gifts. Two things come to mind regarding this:

First, a gift is exactly that… a gift. When given to you, it belongs to you but is empowered by the Spirit to be used for the glory of God, at your discretion. He does not take it away from you.

> *For the gifts and the calling of God are irrevocable.* Romans 11:29

Nor does He force you to use it after He gives it to you. We all must choose what we will do with what the Lord has given us; exercise it and watch it grow and be a blessing, or neglect it and suffer the consequences of the associated lack, as well as having to give an account to Him of our stewardship for what He has entrusted to us.

Secondly, the key thing that the Lord is looking for is *cooperation*. This walk with Him to further His Kingdom is a joint venture. It's a family business of which He wants us to be an integral part. He also wants us to add our uniqueness, sanctified personality, and the creativity that He has put within us to the expression of who He is and what His Kingdom looks like.

This is difficult for many believers to accept because many of us have had a steady church diet of being made to believe that anything in and of ourselves is bad, i.e., "I must die so that He may live.". But that is not exactly so. What needs to die is our flesh, sinful nature, and human reasoning. But what so many people have a hard time believing is that the Father really does like us! He wants an expression of Himself through His kids, just like when one of us, as parents, can see the traits and talents of ourselves in our children. But we also do not want them to be an exact "Mini-Me" replica. Well, maybe some of you who have a narcissistic slant to you want an exact little replica of yourselves running around the house, but trust me—one of me is about all that my family can handle!

In Genesis 2, it says that God brought all the animals to Adam to see what he would name them, and whatever Adam named them, stuck. That shows me that the Lord wanted and cherished Man's input and ideas of what he would come up with. That is the beauty of being a free-willed and thinking sentient being, made in the image of God Himself. I do not believe that God's heart has changed towards us. Of course, with that, and The Fall comes Man's utter ability to break the Father's heart by composing monstrous evils.

Now, with all the gifts of the Spirit, we can position

ourselves to operate in that gift, usually by stepping out in faith and making a demand on that gift to bless someone. In that way, I, the user, am invoking that power at my discretion. But the manifestation does not always come when we step out to use it. From my experience, I cannot choose, at will, to give someone a prophetic word from the Lord. But what I can do is initiate the conversation with the Lord by asking Him if He has a prophetic word for that person. I can also "lean into" my gifting and begin to see if I can see, feel, or sense anything in the spirit that can be used to bless the person. I put my prophetic “antennae” up, so to speak. I do not always get something, but I often do as I make myself available. Thus, I can always try and initiate my prophetic gifting, but it does not always manifest.

It is quite different, though, when you walk into a restaurant, thinking about what you are going to eat, and then you immediately see something in the spirit regarding the person behind the counter when you see them. This is the Lord initiating your prophetic gift.

Let's take another example; say healing, for example. Someone will not get healed if I do not first initiate the encounter or contact. Stewardship entails responsibility. Now, if I see or hear of someone with a sickness, injury, etc., I will initiate laying hands upon them for healing. Some get healed radically, some do not. I do not know 100% of the time that the gift is going to operate when I step out in faith. But I always believe for it too, as I believe that that is what Jesus always wants to do.

However, I do know that when the Holy Spirit initiates the healing gift by giving a prophetic word of knowledge about someone's ailment, or He gives me a vision in the spirit of ministering to someone for healing, or I just know in my spirit that the person needs healing, or I start to feel a fire in the center of my right hand (which is specific to me of how God manifests a healing anointing through me—yours may be different or no manifestation at all), then I know that it will happen.

So, the key difference is positioning ourselves and self-initiating at our discretion, versus God's initiating the use of a spiritual gift. Both are needed and expected, but when He initiates it, you can bank on it manifesting. So, it is with all nine of the spiritual gifts. Though out of the nine spiritual gifts, tongues are unique.

Tongues are a spirit language of which there are four different manifestations. Three of these manifestations are tongues given as a public prophetic word followed by interpretation, tongues of intercession, and tongues spoken as a sign and wonder gift where the speaker is speaking but it is heard in (or can be) a known worldly tongue to people who understand that language, usually foreign to the speaker (as at the Day of Pentecost in Acts 2). These manifestations are all *God-initiated functions* of tongues that we cannot make happen, but we can make ourselves readily available to be a conduit of them as we sense Him leading. Then, we do the actual speaking.

The fourth manifestation or function of tongues is as a personal prayer or spirit language that 7 out of 9 of the benefits listed in this chapter address. What is unique about this aspect of tongues compared to all the other gifts of the Spirit is that YOU can initiate this tongue yourself with 100% success every time.

Tongues, as a spirit/prayer language, manifest every time that you do it, AT WILL. This one exception to all the spiritual gifts is HUGE when it comes to gaining spirit muscle!

Can be used compatibly with music and song. (v.15)

> *What is the conclusion then? I will pray with the spirit, and I will also pray with the understanding. I will sing with the spirit, and I will also sing with the understanding.* 1 Corinthians 14:15

This is self-explanatory. Since tongues are a spirit language, it makes sense that we can also sing in that language. What another beautiful way for His children to be able to express their hearts and the depths of their spirit to Him! Especially for those who are already musically inclined, what a fulfillment of expression that's done in a way He has already gifted you.

This may sound complicated to do, but it's not. You just sing a tune, a melody (say your favorite worship song), but instead of the usual words, you just sing in tongues. Do not worry about what words to say… the Holy Spirit turns what comes out of your spirit, via your mouth, into words. I know it sounds completely counterintuitive, and it has nothing to do with your mind/brain, so stop trying to figure it out. It's a supernatural, spiritual gift. If it were natural, you would not need the Holy Spirit for it. But it is WE who do it.
Just know that once you get the gift of speaking in tongues as a spirit language, then this expression is available to you.

I have a good friend, Larry, who was one of the pastors at a church that I attended. I asked Larry what his encounter was like when he first received tongues. He told me of a church service that he had attended earlier in his life. He said that it was a spirit-filled church where the pastor had directed the congregation into a short time of worshipping/singing "in the Spirit", as a congregation, which was orderly and explained. Now, Larry did not speak in tongues, but he said that when he heard the entire congregation singing in tongues to the Lord, it sounded like angels singing. It was the most beautiful thing that he had ever heard. And the crazy thing was that everyone was singing whatever they wanted to—different tunes and different words, but it all supernaturally blended to bless the Lord directly from their spirits. Larry said that upon hearing that, he wanted to speak in tongues for himself. Shortly thereafter, he received the baptism of the Holy Spirit and tongues and was able to join in.

If you have never experienced an expression of the Church like this, please do so before you get to Heaven, because it is an interlude of Heaven-on-Earth. I believe that angels love to join in with us when we sing in the Spirit. And why wouldn't they? According to Paul, it's in their language!

The ability to give thanks well, directly from your spirit, even when you cannot articulate and put into words what you are feeling. (v.15-17)

> *For if I pray in a tongue, my spirit prays, but my understanding is unfruitful...*
> *For you indeed give thanks well...* 1 Corinthians 14:14,17

This ties in well with praying and singing in the Spirit mentioned above. Notice that Paul states that one who gives thanks in tongues "indeed" gives thanks well. In the context, though, he is saying that during a service, the guy next to you cannot say, "Amen", because he does not understand you. Aside from the point of correction about tongues in a public service, let's mine the gold out of what Paul does say that is positive.

Have you ever been in a situation where you were so overcome with love, joy, gratitude, someone's kindness, or mercy that you could not even put into words what you were feeling? In times like that, "Thank you!" is good, but just repeating it repeatedly still does not seem to be worthy or adequate to express the depths of what you are feeling towards God. How about, "Lord, I love you! No, I really, really, really love you! Sooooo much, I really, really mean it!" Often, you want to express more, but there are no words. Well, in the spirit realm, there are! Whenever I feel this deep affection and gratitude for Him, I express it in tongues. And I must tell you… it is the *only* way that I have found that fulfills and satisfies that release of expression from my heart and spirit, as that is what it was designed to do.

How about debilitating grief or gripping fear? The function of tongues is the same for that as well. When you do not know how to pray, but you know that you should, the Holy Spirit, through tongues, can help you to articulate from the very core of your being, your spirit-man, to God exactly what is going on inside of you. Show me one praying person on the planet, let alone a Christian, who would not think that that is one of the most useful and awesome possibilities that there is regarding prayer. "Deep calls unto deep…" (Ps. 42:7), spirit to Spirit.

A believer speaking in tongues as a personal prayer/praise spirit language is not only receiving and making use of a gift ***from*** God, but they can return it as a gift ***to*** God! Beautiful.

I've witnessed the power and beauty of this firsthand in the saints. We were conducting a meeting where three women had not yet received the baptism of the Holy Spirit with speaking in tongues, and they all wanted it.

Before we laid hands on them to receive it, I explained to them exactly what was going to happen and in what way they needed to cooperate with Him to step into receiving their prayer language. I told them that praying in tongues was their ***intimate love language*** to Him, which expresses the deepest parts of themselves to Him by their spirit.

As soon as one of the women heard this, she immediately threw up her hands and began crying out in tongues through tears as the Spirit of God fell upon her in power. We didn't even need to lay hands on her because when she heard that there was a closer and more intimate encounter with her Lord than what she currently had, she was not going to wait another moment. Upon seeing this, it was nothing for the other two ladies to receive their baptism in the Holy Spirit with speaking in tongues immediately after.

The opportunity to be a miraculous sign to unbelievers when you speak or are interpreted as a known human language that you do not know or comprehend. (v.22)

> *Therefore, tongues are for a* ***sign****, not to those who believe but to unbelievers...* 1 Corinthians 14:22

A believer can speak in tongues, and it can manifest, or be heard, as a known language in the world, yet that language would be unknown to the one speaking it. I have witnessed this and heard many stories of a third-party person hearing the language being spoken and understanding what was being said as if it were their native language. This one manifestation of tongues is called tongues as a *sign & wonder gift*.

The Day of Pentecost, in Acts 2, is where we have the first and most famous example of tongues as a sign & wonder gift. There, we see Jesus' first 120 disciples being filled with the Holy Spirit, praising and prophesying in their spirit language as they spill out onto the street from the upper room. As this was happening, the surrounding crowd heard them each in their language, and this was a miraculous sign to them that something supernatural from heaven was taking place.

Now, the assumption that we make is that the entire 120 believers are speaking in known human languages, but I believe this incorrect assumption has led us to other incorrect doctrinal views. I will unpack this topic in detail in the next chapter, Chapter 5, *Was the Purpose of Tongues for Preaching the Gospel in Other Languages?*

So, there you have it—a myriad of benefits. I hope that as you study, meditate on, and discuss the gift of tongues, your perspective has shifted from one that might have been negative and suspicious to one that recognizes the true blessing of God that it is meant to be for us —and sometimes, for others.

Chapter Five

"Was the Purpose of Tongues for Preaching the Gospel in Other Languages?"

The Miracle Was in the Hearing

The viewpoint that God's purpose for speaking in tongues was to enable the early Church to preach the gospel in other known human languages is the traditional belief. This faulty premise has resulted in many in the Body believing that, because we now have the written Scriptures and modern communication/interpretation methods, we no longer need the gift of speaking in tongues. This is patently false—and I'll prove it—through the text of Scripture, logic, basic physics, and common sense.

First, I have a confession to make. When I began writing this book, I believed that on the Day of Pentecost in Acts 2, the 120 disciples spoke in other known human languages. I subscribed to, like most other people, this accepted, traditional viewpoint. But I also knew from firsthand experience through receiving the baptism of the Holy Spirit with the gift of speaking in tongues, that the primary purpose and use of tongues was *not* for communicating to other people groups via a human language that is unknown to the speaker, but is primarily for connecting to God by the Spirit.

Throughout 1 Corinthians 14, Paul interchanges the terms "*speaking in tongues*" and "*praying in tongues*" multiple times, even inferring that he prays/speaks, and even sings to God in tongues himself. So, this should easily resolve any argument that there is no such thing as tongues as a personal prayer or spirit language. Paul's comments clearly refute this.

As I wrote this book, I also sought the Lord for His guidance in bringing clarity to His people regarding this subject, specifically, and was open to anything He wanted to reveal to me. As I reread the events of Acts 2, I was stunned that the scripture never actually states that the disciples were speaking in other human languages!

Let's begin by re-reading it:

> *When the Day of Pentecost had fully come, they were all with one accord in one place. [2] And suddenly there came a sound from heaven, as of a rushing mighty wind, and it filled the whole house where they were sitting. [3] Then there appeared to them divided tongues, as of fire, and one sat upon each of them. [4] And they were all filled with the Holy Spirit and began to speak with other tongues, as the Spirit gave them utterance. [5] And there were dwelling in Jerusalem Jews, devout men, from every nation under heaven. [6] And when this sound occurred, the multitude came together, and were confused,* ***because everyone <u>heard</u> <u>them</u>*** *speak in* ***<u>his</u>***

> ***own* language**. [7] *Then they were all amazed and marveled, saying to one another, "Look, are not all these who speak Galileans?* [8] *And how is it that* ***we hear, each in our own language*** *in which we were born?* [9] *Parthians and Medes and Elamites, those dwelling in Mesopotamia, Judea and Cappadocia, Pontus and Asia,* [10] *Phrygia and Pamphylia, Egypt and the parts of Libya adjoining Cyrene, visitors from Rome, both Jews and proselytes,* [11] *Cretans and Arabs—****we hear them speaking in our own tongues*** *the wonderful works of God."* [12] *So they were all amazed and perplexed, saying to one another, "Whatever could this mean?"* Acts 2:1-12

You see, it never says that they were speaking in other known languages, yet that's what we assume. It says that they were speaking *"with other tongues,"* which typically and biblically is the first thing that happens when someone is baptized with the Holy Spirit in power and the recipient receives their spirit/prayer language.

The verse says that the crowd *"**heard them** in their **own languages**."* That is so significant. The miracle was in the hearing and not the speaking. My jaw hit the floor because, like most people, I had assumed a presumption about what the text meant instead of what the text *actually says*. And, because I understand how tongues work from years of using them in their different functions, this made much more sense than the traditional viewpoint. A viewpoint that is mainly espoused by people who do not even speak in tongues; thus, they would have no other basis by which to come to a different conclusion.

One of the principles of good biblical hermeneutics (the theory and methodology of scriptural text interpretation) is to, whenever possible, use Scripture to confirm Scripture. With this in mind, we see that the event on the Day of Pentecost was not the first time a supernatural sign involved hearing.

> *Father, glorify Your name." Then a voice came from heaven, saying, "I have both glorified it and will glorify it again."* [29] *Therefore the people who stood by and heard it said that it had thundered. Others said, "An angel has spoken to Him."* [30] *Jesus answered and said, "This voice did not come because of Me,* ***but for your sake.*** John 12:28-30

> *Then a voice came from heaven, "You are My beloved Son, in whom I am well pleased."* Mark 1:11; Luke 3:22; Matthew 3:17

> *While he was still speaking, behold, a bright cloud overshadowed them; and suddenly a voice came out of the cloud, saying, "This is My beloved Son, in whom I am well pleased. Hear Him!"* Matthew 17:5

In these examples, we see miraculous signs involving hearing. In the first example from John, the hearing was supernaturally granted in varying degrees of clarity—to some, but not to others—*"he who has ears to hear, let him hear"*, was a common theme and principle of Jesus' ministry. Hearing had a direct correlation to one's heart posture. The miracle of a manifested voice happened, but how and what was heard was dependent on the person and designated accordingly by God in His sovereignty.

Additionally, there are further clues from the text that back up this assertion:

> [6] *And when this sound occurred, the multitude came together, and were confused, because* ***everyone heard them speak in his own language***.

v. 6 This says that everyone in the multitude, who were from every nation under heaven, heard **"them"** (plural) speak **"his own"** (singular) language. This simply states that each individual heard their own native language emerge from **all** the 120 disciples collectively.

> [7] *Then they were all amazed and marveled, saying to one another, "Look, are not* ***all these who speak Galileans****?* [8] *And how is it that we hear,* ***each in our own language*** *in which we were born?*

So, another way to phrase this verse from what the Greek text says is:

> "Then the entire crowd was amazed and marveled, saying one to another, 'Look, are not all these 120 people who are speaking Galileans? And how is it that ***each one of us*** is hearing ***all*** of them speak in the language of each of our respective homelands?"

v.7-8 The reason why this was so amazing was not only that a group of Galileans would be speaking any other language other than Aramaic or Hebrew, but that it was an even greater miracle that if within a multitude of people, standing next to each other, **"each"** heard the 120 Galileans (foreigners to the hearers) collectively speaking their own language! The conversation between those present could have gone something like this:

"Hey, what's up with all of these crazy Parthians?"

"Parthians? No, they're not. They're Cappadocian! They're speaking Cappadocian."

"Cappadocian? No, my friend, that's Egyptian! In fact, it's the specific dialect from my region."

And from yet another, "Nope, it's Latin! I'm visiting from Rome, and that's Latin. Why would these Jewish brothers be speaking in the language of Rome!?!"

"Look, are not all these who speak Galileans? How is it that we each hear them speaking in our own native languages, the wonderful works of God? "

"Hey, you're right. They are Galileans! How is this possible? Whatever could this mean?"

> *...*[11] *—we hear them speaking in our own tongues the wonderful works of God."* [12] *So they were all amazed and perplexed, saying to one another, "Whatever could this mean?"*

This is an example of what the Apostle Paul meant when he describes speaking in tongues when it manifests as a sign & wonder gift, which I first mentioned in the table in Chapter 3 (p. 31) as one of the benefits, or manifestations of tongues.

> *Therefore, tongues are for a sign, not to those who believe but to unbelievers...* 1 Corinthians 14:22

The impartation of their prayer/spirit language upon their baptism of the Holy Spirit was what the disciples were experiencing for themselves, but it was sovereignly manifesting as praise and prophesying that was heard and understood by unbelievers as a sign that made them wonder.

If They Were Speaking in Known Human Languages, Just Consider the Physics!

I believe that each of us, as we read the stories contained in Scripture, imagines or envisages what that scenario would have looked like had we been standing amid it. The only problem with that is that if we do not get the details of the story correct, we may find ourselves painting a mental picture of the event or story that leads us to a wrong conclusion because "we've always imagined it that way". I believe that is exactly what most people have done with the Day of Pentecost in Acts 2. And this is where the reality of physics, specifically *spatial acoustics*, comes into play. Don't worry; I'm not going to get all scientific on you.

Remember, this was Jerusalem at the time of one of the required pilgrimage feasts, the Feast of Weeks (Pentecost). The city was crowded by *"Jews, devout men, from every nation under heaven."(v.5)*. When the sound from heaven came as a rushing mighty wind and filled the house of the upper room, resulting in the 120 disciple's infilling of the Holy Spirit and power with the subsequent praise and prophesying that was heard in every language, the bible says that the *multitude* came together to see what this was.

Now we know that shortly thereafter, the Apostle Peter addresses that same crowd, and three thousand people get saved. Even if that was every single person in the multitude, that would still be a lot of people on the street. And since we can assume that not every person there responded to Peter's call to repentance, it would be safe to say that there may have been *well over* 3,000 people present.

Now I want you to picture a busy Jerusalem street during this festival with thousands of people. Now, add the 120 disciples with all their exuberant supernatural behavior. Can you imagine the noise? The acoustics of this in, light of the reality of the sheer numbers of people along with the accompanying myriads of street sounds and voices, would be overwhelming, let alone for the one person who spoke Arabic who was somewhere within the multitude, to be able to pick out and hear the one or even a few disciples, out of the 120, who were speaking Arabic amidst the cacophony of other languages! This is highly unlikely, if not impossible.

However, if that one person within the multitude who spoke Arabic heard all 120 of these Galileans proclaiming the wonders of God in Arabic, then the chances are increased exponentially that, regardless of how far away he was from them, he would have been able to recognize what was happening and being proclaimed. So, it would also be for every other visiting Jewish foreigner on that day. This is just a logical conclusion if we were to be present at this event and consider practically the surroundings described.

When making this point in a congregation, it is very easy to demonstrate this fact while only using ten people up in front of the congregation, speaking only three or four languages simultaneously. It is difficult, if not impossible, to understand or pick out anything that is being said by any one individual, let alone if we added another 110 people speaking another dozen languages. It's just not practically feasible when considering the number of people, the surroundings, the acoustics, and the spatial relationships within this mass of people.

Thus, the supposition that the purpose for tongues being given by God on the Day of Pentecost was primarily for the saints to preach the gospel in other known human languages is not supported by the text itself or the physical realities surrounding what was described. This assertion is further proved correct when we look at what happened *immediately after* the 120 spilled out onto the streets.

Further Proof That the Gift of Tongues Was Not for Preaching the Gospel

The circus-like atmosphere that I described above is further proven by the fact that the disciples were accused of drunkenness—"*Others mocking said, 'They are full of new wine.'" v.13.* Let's be honest, preaching a sermon does not garner this kind of accusation. Even street preachers, though being heckled, hated, or argued against, are not accused of drunkenness, which has a noticeably physical element to it.

For me, the greatest proof that speaking in tongues was not for the preaching of the Gospel is the fact that immediately after all these events happened, and the disciples now had the attention of thousands of onlookers, Peter stood up and **then preached the Gospel** for the next twenty-seven verses in Aramaic! (Acts 2:14-41)

This was the common language spoken by Jesus and throughout Israel. So why would Peter need to then step up and first give clarity as to what was happening by referencing the prophet Joel's prophecy of the Lord *"pouring out His Spirit upon all flesh"*? Peter explained and gave context to the question, "*Whatever could this mean?*" He did this because the purpose of miraculous signs and wonders is to point to a greater reality—the Gospel. Signs and wonders are used to both announce and confirm the message that accompanies them. They're not the entrée, but the appetizer and dessert. Some have said that "Signs and wonders are the dinner bell for the Gospel."

The tongues spoken by the 120 were a sign and wonder billboard that set the stage for Peter's preaching of the Gospel!

More Proof – Peter Preaching the Gospel: The Sequel

How about the next time we hear about Peter preaching the Gospel? In Acts 10, we see him in Joppa, Israel, at Cornelius the Centurion's house. Gathered there were all Cornelius's relatives and close friends, all Gentiles. Peter began preaching to them. However, when they heard the Gospel, the Holy Spirit fell on them in power, and all the Gentiles began to "*speak in tongues and magnify God*". For what foreigners were these new Gentile converts speaking in tongues? If tongues are for the communication of the Gospel, in known human languages, then where are they? Only friends and family here. What do you need tongues for then? Unless… it was them getting their spirit language with which to connect with and magnify God.

Even More Proof – Did Paul Need Tongues for His Missions?

One of the arguments made by those who believe that the spiritual gift of tongues was given to facilitate communication of the Gospel with people of other languages is connected to the Apostle Paul's missionary journeys into Asia Minor and Macedonia. They say that Paul needed the spiritual gift of tongues to be able to miraculously communicate with the Gentiles in these regions. They believe this is why Paul states in 1 Corinthians 14:18-19,

> ***I thank my God I speak with tongues more than you all;*** 19 *yet in the church I would rather speak five words with my understanding, that I may teach others also, than ten thousand words in a tongue.*

Subsequently, Paul needed to use this gift often because of all his travels to different people groups where he planted churches. However, this viewpoint has four problems:

First, in the time of Alexander the Great, a Macedonian King, he conquered all the lands from Greece to Egypt to India, including the Holy Land. By the time of Jesus and Paul, Greek had been the main language of learning, commerce, and administration for four hundred years! Though languages and dialects of particular people groups were still spoken, most of the Mediterranean and Middle Eastern world knew Greek. Why do you think that the New Testament was written in Greek? Because it was *the* language that everyone was familiar with and understood. God had this for His timing of the Gospel going forth into the world.

Secondly, if this gift was primarily for translation and communication purposes, then why would Paul state in verse nineteen (above) that "*in the church*" he doesn't want tongues being spoken openly, but in the known language of understanding? How could he speak any words of understanding in the church service if he didn't know the language? Wouldn't it necessitate that he speak in tongues the entire church service to "*teach others*" about the Gospel, using at least "*ten thousand words*"?

Thirdly, in 1 Corinthians 13:1, he states, "*Though I speak with the tongues of men* ***and*** *of angels, but have not love...*". So, Paul is clearly stating that there are the tongues of men, known languages, and the tongues of angels, spiritual languages, which a person can speak.

And finally, to drive the final nail into the coffin of this argument, Paul specifically states in 1 Corinthians 14:2,

> *For he who speaks in a tongue* ***does not speak to men but to God****, for no one understands him; however,* ***in the spirit*** *he speaks mysteries.*

I don't believe that it gets any clearer than that. Speaking in tongues is not for or to other people in human languages. It is a spirit language of connection to the Lord, that He may, upon His initiative, manifest as a sign and wonder for another person to understand.

More Recent Proof – An Incorrect Pentecostal Assumption of the Past

In the early days of the Pentecostal Movement (the early 1900's), when the Lord began restoring to the Church at large the biblical truths of both the baptism of the Holy Spirit (BOTHS), speaking in tongues, and the supernatural gifts of the Spirit, those that received it then tried to hammer-out the specific theology behind what they were experiencing.

The first person in the movement (before it was a movement, it was just a Bible school) to receive this experience was Agnes Ozman, in Topeka, Kansas, in 1901. When she received the BOTHS, she began to speak in tongues, which they all believed was a Chinese dialect. It was purported that for three days following, she could not speak or write in English, but only in this Chinese-sounding language. Her language and writings, which were just scribblings, were never verified as actual Chinese because, as we know now, speaking the actual Chinese language was not its purpose.

Because of the traditional reading, assumption, and understanding of Acts 2 that I detailed previously, coupled with a lack of first-hand experience and understanding of the gift of tongues, there came into use the term "mission tongues". By limiting tongues to solely the manifestation of only a *sign & wonder gift*, based on an incorrect presumptive reading of Acts 2, Pentecostals began to extrapolate that if the tongues that you received upon receiving the BOTHS sounded like an existing, known human language, then that must mean that you are called to go and be a witness or missionary to that people group. This was one of the reasons why the Pentecostal experience began sweeping very quickly throughout the Church worldwide. They went, even with this wrong understanding.

But there was the assumption that a person with said tongues would go to that nation or people and begin praying in tongues openly, and that everyone within its hearing would understand and come to Jesus. As I am sure there may have been an extremely rare singular occurrence when this may have worked, this was not the case and caused significant hardship and discouragement to those who were not prepared for or even called to the foreign mission field.

In the early 1900's, an investigative article on this specific issue was done by S. C. Todd of the Bible Missionary Society and is summarized as follows:

[Missionaries were soon sent, dispatched to places such as Japan, China, and India. At the time, the more mainstream Bible Missionary Society investigated eighteen Pentecostal missionaries to see how they were faring. Not one of them reported being able to communicate successfully with those to whom they were sent. Tongue-speaking evangelism wasn't working.][2]

This is no surprise to those of us who have spoken in tongues both as a private spirit language and as a public ministry gift. When you operate in it and study its theology, you come to realize that there are variations of the manifestation of tongues, but they are all rooted in our personal prayer/spirit language. It is important to walk with the Holy Spirit in discerning the different manifestations, and thus the various purposes of each—remember it is called *various* or *varieties of tongues*, <u>not</u> referring to various known human languages.

What we see both today, and in Scripture of the occurrences of the saints receiving the BOTHS—the Day of Pentecost, Cornelius' household, the Ephesian twelve, etc., is that each person received the ability to pray/praise in a spirit language which was primarily given as a gift for themselves (and never taken away) and sometimes was used by God for an additional purpose, i.e. sign & wonder, or a prophetic word/utterance in a meeting, but never as a primary evangelistic tool for preaching the gospel.

Because of this faulty assumption regarding the purpose of speaking in tongues, paired with only anecdotal modern-day evidence of it having any evangelistic application, it is no wonder that this misconception has caused so many believers to dismiss this gift altogether as not needed, because they're primarily expecting it to be something that it's not.

---

[2] **Early Pentecostal Speaking in Tongues was About Foreign Languages -** Fr. Andrew Stephen Damick April 12, 2016

Modern-Day Manifestation of Tongues as a Sign?

I heard a story from a minister with whom I am familiar, who went down to Mexico for a ministry trip. Through some unfortunate turn of events, the translator that she had planned to assist her was not available when she was in a village to preach. She felt like the Holy Spirit told her to just start speaking in tongues. She did, and to her amazement, everyone was listening to her as if they could understand everything that she was saying. So, she kept going until she felt like the Spirit was done, which was about twenty minutes or so. This woman lives in Arizona, so she would be familiar with what Spanish sounds like, and she knew that it was not Spanish, but it was just her personal tongue, which was manifested as a sign gift by the Lord. It's something to consider.

Though also rare, I also believe that there may have been those who, when speaking in their spirit language, have spoken in a known language that they do not naturally know, but it is a human language. What a sign to someone who speaks that language! Sometimes, God will give a prophetic word through a tongue, in a language that only one person in the place or meeting understands, and the prophetic word is that which is specifically pertinent to only that one person in the room who can speak the language. Talk about a confirmation that God wants to tell you something.

God can do anything He wants with what we give Him when submitting to His Spirit. My suggestion is to be open and available to Him for anything and leave the results to Him.

Modern-Day Manifestation of Tongues of Intercession?

I was preparing for a trip to several African nations, including South Sudan. There, I was going to teach the Army Chaplains Corps of the South Sudan People's Defense Forces about the baptism of the Holy Spirit and power. Going to this nation was very dangerous and required much prayer and intercession leading up to the trip. During our local regional prayer meetings for the two months leading up to my trip, my prayer language changed. All the intercessors who were there noticed that it began to change from my usual tongue. It sounded more Arabic, and I noticed myself saying something sounding like "Allah" very often. At the time, I did not give it much thought.

However, when we finally arrived in South Sudan as our third nation to visit, I discovered upon meeting my translator that Arabic was the language spoken there. The Arabic word for God is "Allah" and is used in Arabic when referring to God, whether in Islam, Judaism, or Christianity. I then realized that the Lord was guiding my intercession during the months before my time in the nation. During those times, I may have or may not have been praying in Arabic; it really doesn't matter. What did matter was that I was praying out the mysteries of God by the Spirit.

Many people get caught up in trying to figure out what exactly they are praying for to find some significance when the sound of the language changes. I do not. Why not? Because it's a spirit language, from my spirit, being guided by the Holy Spirit. If He wants or needs to tell me what I am praying, He will give me an interpretation *if* it's even necessary. But I am primarily focused on communing with Him in prayer, completely by faith, trusting that I am there as a vessel and am on a need-to-know basis.

What's the Purpose? It's Just a Hug from My Dad.

I knew a woman who, whenever she spoke in tongues, sounded like some French dialect. I'm not saying that it was, but it sure sounded very much like it. I have a university minor in French along with my degree in International Business, and I thought that it sounded so amazing, but I couldn't understand any of it. So, I asked the Lord, "Lord, I went to school and paid to learn this, and I can barely speak it. And here is this woman who has it as her regular prayer language. I think that is so cool and I really want it!" So, for the next two weeks after I had asked Him for it, every time I would speak in tongues, it was that same French-sounding tongue. After two weeks, it went back to my usual sounding tongue. Bummer. But the Father is so good to be so personally gracious like that.

> *Delight yourself also in the Lord, and He shall give you the desires of your heart.* Psalm 37:4

Many people have commented that my prayer tongue sounds like Hebrew, and most often, it does, but I do not believe it is Hebrew. Depending on the moment and spiritual circumstances, my tongue has sounded like many different languages: Swedish, Russian, Burmese, Vietnamese, Native American, Arabic, and many others. In all these times, however, communication with others was not the purpose—pressing into the Spirit of God and praying out His mysteries was the purpose.

Chapter Six

"I Thought the Bible Says That Not Everyone Can Speak in Tongues?"

FOR EASE OF REFERENCE

1 Corinthians 12 (NKJV)

Spiritual Gifts: Unity in Diversity

12 *Now concerning spiritual gifts, brethren, I do not want*
you to be ignorant: 2 *You know that you were Gentiles,*
carried away to these dumb idols, however you were led.
3 *Therefore I make known to you that no one speaking by the*
Spirit of God calls Jesus accursed, and no one can say that
Jesus is Lord except by the Holy Spirit.
4 *There are diversities of gifts, but the same Spirit.* 5 *There are*
differences of ministries, but the same Lord. 6 *And there are*
diversities of activities, but it is the same God who works all in
all. 7 *But the manifestation of the Spirit is given to each one for*
the profit of all: 8 *for to one is given the word of wisdom through*
the Spirit, to another the word of knowledge through the same
Spirit, 9 *to another faith by the same Spirit, to another gifts of*
healings by the same Spirit, 10 *to another the working of*

miracles, to another prophecy, to another discerning of spirits, to another different kinds of tongues, to another the interpretation of tongues. [11] But one and the same Spirit works all these things, distributing to each one individually as He wills.

Unity and Diversity in One Body

[12] For as the body is one and has many members, but all the members of that one body, being many, are one body, so also is Christ. [13] For by one Spirit we were all baptized into one body—whether Jews or Greeks, whether slaves or free—and have all been made to drink into one Spirit. [14] For in fact the body is not one member but many.

[15] If the foot should say, "Because I am not a hand, I am not of the body," is it therefore not of the body? [16] And if the ear should say, "Because I am not an eye, I am not of the body," is it therefore not of the body? [17] If the whole body were an eye, where would be the hearing? If the whole were hearing, where would be the smelling? [18] But now God has set the members, each one of them, in the body just as He pleased. [19] And if they were all one member, where would the body be?

[20] But now indeed there are many members, yet one body. [21] And the eye cannot say to the hand, "I have no need of you"; nor again the head to the feet, "I have no need of you."

[22] No, much rather, those members of the body which seem to be weaker are necessary. [23] And those members of the body which we think to be less honorable, on these we bestow greater honor; and our unpresentable parts have greater modesty, [24] but our presentable parts have no need. But God composed the body, having given greater honor to that part which lacks it, [25] that there should be no schism in the body, but that the members should have the same care for one another. [26] And if one member suffers, all the members suffer with it; or if one member is honored, all the members rejoice with it.

[27] Now you are the body of Christ, and members individually. [28] And God has appointed these in the church: first apostles, second prophets, third teachers, after that miracles, then gifts of healings, helps, administrations, varieties of tongues. [29] Are all apostles? Are all prophets? Are all teachers? Are all workers of miracles? [30] Do all have gifts of healings? Do all speak with tongues? Do all interpret? [31] But earnestly desire the best gifts. And yet I show you a more excellent way.

Fostering Honor, Respect & Unity; Not Disqualification

This chapter is by far the most challenging, as it is the most used objection that most Christians cite in *disqualifying themselves* from operating in tongues. In order to completely dismantle any and all obstacles that would hinder you from receiving the gift of tongues, let's cover many different aspects that may seem peripheral but are essential in helping to free you from any theological objections and/or doubts.

First, let's look at the text:

> *And God has appointed these in the church: first apostles, second prophets, third teachers, after that miracles, then gifts of healings, helps, administrations, varieties of tongues. [29] Are all apostles? Are all prophets? Are all teachers? Are all workers of miracles? [30] Do all have gifts of healings?* ***Do all speak with tongues?*** *Do all interpret?* 1 Corinthians 12:28-30

For context, Paul is discussing in the entire twelfth chapter of First Corinthians the fact that the Church Body is made up of many different types of people with a diversity of gifts, callings, and ministries entrusted to them by God. However, even though there is such variety, the acts are all done by the same Holy Spirit through each individual. Paul's ultimate reason and point for writing this chapter is to show that *we all need each other* and thus should honor and value what each of us brings to the table without trying to mimic or compete with one another. Therefore, in context, the final questions that he is posing have a presupposed answer of "No." Do all speak with tongues? No. Do all have the same callings and ministry gifts? No.

Verse 30 has invariably been used by untold multitudes of Christians to explain why they do not have the gift of speaking in tongues. At face value, this would seem obvious. But we have other verses and examples throughout the New Testament that would hint at a different reality and possibility. A careful examination of his statements will show that there is more to this and that we should not base an entire doctrine on one statement that was not the intended purpose of the entire chapter. Paul was not penning 1 Corinthians 12 to show everyone that they do not have access to any or all of the spiritual powers that are manifested through the spiritual gifts. And, I guarantee that he also did not intend to use his one statement as a biblical excuse to not have the faith, nor the desire, to enter into any of them. We know this because later he states, "I wish that you all spoke in tongues…"(v.5), and "I thank my God I speak with tongues more than you all…" (v.18), meaning that he sees a need, relevance, and benefit of everyone exercising it.

When Bible Verses Seem Contradictory

I want to talk generally about the different times that biblical authors have written things that have *seemed* completely contradictory to one another. There are several instances throughout Scripture where these conflicting texts have caused people to doubt the validity of the written Word as being divinely inspired.

I know that most of us have heard the charge, "The Bible is full of contradictions," leveled by atheists and agnostics alike. What those who believe this way do not understand is that God is trying to get us to see the subtle perfection of understanding the *exact nuances* of the truth that He is prescribing. If something in Scripture initially seems contradictory, but you do not give up seeking the answer to the "whys" behind them, because you know that God is not a man that He should lie, then you will receive an understanding of the perfect answer. That is called revelation.

Let's look at an example in the Bible that seems to offer two contradictory viewpoints about the same issue. The Apostle Paul states:

> *For by grace you have been saved* ***through faith, and that not of yourselves****; it is the gift of God,* [9]***<u>not of works</u>****, lest anyone should boast.* [10]*For we are His workmanship, created in Christ Jesus for good works, which God prepared beforehand that we should walk in them.* Ephesians 2:8-10

> *For* ***<u>if</u> Abraham <u>was justified by works</u>, he has something to boast about****, but not before God.* [3]*For what does the Scripture say? "Abraham believed God, and it was accounted to him for righteousness."* [4]*Now to him who works, the wages are not counted as grace but as debt.*[5] ***But to him who does not work but believes on Him*** *who justifies the ungodly,* ***his faith is accounted for righteousness****,* [6]*just as David also describes the*

blessedness of the man to whom ***God imputes righteousness <u>apart from works</u>****...* Romans 4:2-6

Then, James, the brother of Jesus Christ himself, and a prominent leader in the Jerusalem church, writes:

> *Thus also* ***<u>faith by itself, if it does not have works, is dead.</u>*** [18] *But someone will say, "You have faith, and I have works." Show me your faith without your works, and I will show you my faith by my works.* [19] *You believe that there is one God. You do well. Even the demons believe—and tremble!* [20] *But do you want to know, O foolish man,* ***<u>that faith without works is dead</u>****?* [21] ***<u>Was not Abraham our father justified by works</u>*** *when he offered Isaac his son on the altar?* [22] *Do you see that faith was working together with his works,* ***and by works faith was made perfect****?* [23] *And the Scripture was fulfilled which says, "Abraham believed God, and it was accounted to him for righteousness." And he was called the friend of God.* [24] ***You see then that <u>a man is justified by works, and not by faith only</u>.*** James 2:17-24

Do you see how these verses, at face value, seem completely contradictory? But they are not. They both quote a verse from Genesis 15:6 to prove their seemingly opposite points. These two verses were a major stumbling block to both Catholics and Protestants during the Reformation and Counter-Reformation eras. If you did not pursue further understanding with an openness of heart, you would not see the full revelation that contains both ideas. The longer that you walk with the Lord, and the more that you recognize what the truths of His Kingdom and His Word entail through your experiences and learning with Him, you discover *exactly* what He meant through both of these inspired men of God. Both considerations bring you to the point of the subtle, perfect understanding of receiving imputed, workless, justifying faith that *must* produce righteous works validating the true substance of that faith. Simply said, true, undeserved grace of God, planted in good soil, will always produce fruit. There is always life in a seed that proves it's a true seed by what it produces.

Other examples:

Example #1

- 1 John 3:6-9 *Whoever abides in Him* ***does not sin.*** ***Whoever sins has neither seen Him nor known Him.*** [7] *Little children, let no one deceive you. He who practices righteousness is righteous, just as He is righteous.* [8] ***He who sins is of the devil,*** *for the devil has sinned from the beginning. For this purpose the Son of God was manifested, that He might destroy the works of the devil.* [9] ***Whoever has been born of God does not sin,*** *for His seed remains in him;* ***and he cannot sin, because he has been born of God.***

So, from this verse (alone, at face value), can we say that any one of our Christian brethren, or pastors/leaders, who commits a sin is not saved? Well, that's what this verse says… it says that they are "of the devil" because a born-again Christian ***cannot*** sin. So let's make a doctrine out of that. Or, is there something more that is meant? A subtle perfection, or tension, to what the Apostle John is saying in light of other portions and truths of Scripture.

Example #2

- Luke 14:26 *"If anyone comes to Me and* ***does not hate*** *his father and mother, wife and children,* *brothers and sisters, yes, and his own life also,* ***he cannot be My disciple.*** *" - Jesus*

Obviously, Jesus is using hyperbole here. There's a deeper intention, or subtle perfection, to this statement. If taken literally, it would fly in the face of the meta-narrative of the entire Bible, and specifically, the ministry of Jesus Christ.

Example #3

- 1 Corinthians 11:5-6, 13 *But* ***every woman who prays or prophesies with her head uncovered*** *dishonors her head—it is the same as having her head shaved.* [6] ***For if a woman does not cover her head****, she might as well have her hair cut off; but if* ***it is a disgrace for a woman to have her hair cut off or her head shaved****, then she should cover her head...* [13] *Judge for yourselves***:** ***Is it proper for a woman to pray to God with her head uncovered****?* *NIV*

So, where does that leave you ladies who have short hair, which today, represents most women in the Church over 60 years old? How about those going through radiation treatment for cancer who have no hair at all? Are they disgraceful? Please.

Example #4

- 1 Corinthians 14:35 *And if they* (women) *want to learn something, let them ask their own husbands at home; for* ***it is shameful for women to speak in church****.* *(parentheses added)*

So *(cough)*. Uhhmmm… need I bother?

Instruction Manual or Autobiography?

> *It is the glory of God to* ***conceal a matter****, But the glory of kings is* ***to search out a matter****.* Proverbs 25:2

Also, there are things in the Bible that are not spelled out clearly to completion—on purpose. The Lord will often give us a small taste of an aspect of the Kingdom that He has only sparsely mentioned in the Scriptures, but will only reveal more to us as we walk with Him to discover more about the given topic, under His guidance. Through this relational discipleship, we learn the nuances, exactness, and completeness of various truths that are beyond the scope of what is plainly written in the Bible about some specific topics. But those revealed truths will never be contrary to the heart and spirit of the Word and its overall message.

An example of this is the ministry of deliverance, or the casting out of demons from a person. The Bible gives us several accounts of Jesus and one account of Paul performing deliverance on a person. From these accounts, there are some basic truth nuggets that we can mine. Today, you can find numerous books on the deliverance ministry that have been authored by disciples who have walked with the Lord in this type of ministry over the years. There is a ton of additional information and wisdom that these saints have added to the basic truths in the Scriptures, yet these additions are not in contradiction to them. These additions bring greater clarity, wisdom, and effectiveness to them. They are learned from experience and relational discipleship from the Holy Spirit Himself, while actually doing the works.

If you are engaged in this ministry (let alone your entire Christian walk) using the Bible as an instruction manual instead of an autobiographical guide, you will live a life for God from a perspective of following biblical formulas instead of being led by personal discipleship by "the Spirit of truth who leads and guides you into all truth." So, do we manifest this reality when we often say, "Well, Christianity is not a religion, it's a relationship!"?

There are deeper things that He only reveals to us as we walk with Him in faith, hunger, and openness to the Holy Spirit. Let's see how this truth played out in people performing the deliverance ministry by using a biblical formula, instead of a personal Holy Spirit relationship, in Paul's day:

> *Then some of the itinerant Jewish exorcists* ***took it upon themselves*** *over those who had evil spirits, saying, "We exorcise you by* ***the Jesus whom Paul preaches****."* [14] *Also there were seven sons of Sceva, a Jewish chief priest, who did so.* [15] *And the evil spirit answered and said,* ***"Jesus I know, and Paul I know; but who are you?"*** [16] *Then the man in whom the evil spirit was leaped on them, overpowered them, and prevailed against them, so that they fled out of that house naked and wounded.* Acts 19:13-16

This anecdote shows the marked difference between someone who is functioning in a Kingdom/biblical truth out of the knowledge of information and a formula, versus the fruit of knowledge that comes from an intimate relationship. The Lord never intended for us to take on the demonic realm solely armed with information. He leads and guides us into confronting these realms out of personal revelation. To engage otherwise is obviously dangerous. This is why He does not give us the full written "download" on certain scriptural truths, as He knows that men will take the information or formulae, and just plug them in and expect them to work to obtain God-results... without His Spirit being needed.

That's not to say there aren't biblical principles that the ungodly can put into practice that won't bear fruit for them. There are. But, when it comes to the supernatural/spirit realm, including the spiritual gifts, you do not want to be functioning outside of the leadership and abiding presence of the Holy Spirit.

Now, I want to take this truth and apply this to not only tongues but to all of the spiritual gifts. The Father does not give you all of your gifts like it was Christmas morning, and then say, "Run along outside with your friends, Bobby, and play baseball with your new glove." Or, "Have fun using your new tea set, Cindy." No. He says, "Hey Bobby, get your new glove, and let's go outside and play catch!" Or "Cindy, My love, where's Daddy's seat at your tea party?"

Quite simply, there are nuances and truths that you will *never* come to a complete understanding of unless you experience them for yourself. This is true of being born again. This is true of receiving the baptism of the Holy Spirit. This is true of deliverance. This is true of all of the spiritual gifts. This is true of speaking in tongues. Let's explore one of those realizations about tongues next.

Understanding the Different Kinds of Tongues

Most people come to realize after they have operated in tongues that the gift of tongues they received upon their baptism of the Holy Spirit is primarily a personal prayer language for private use. Tongues also give them the ability to intercede when the Holy Spirit provides the unction. But most have never experienced the other two manifestations, which are exclusively for use in public ministry: as a *sign & wonder gift* or a *prophetic gift*. It would seem wise to consider the possibility of the existence of various types of tongues if it's being espoused by actual tongue speakers. That it is not only possible but backed up by scriptural examples and verses.

Since the night I received the baptism of the Holy Spirit with tongues decades ago, I have discovered not only the different types of tongues but the parameters by which they work or are initiated. Although they all have different functions, they all still flow out of the operation of a believer's granted spirit language that they receive upon their infilling of the Spirit in power.

Privately, as a prayer/praise language, I use tongues daily. I have been led by the Spirit into those same tongues, for supernatural intercession, countless times. Only once, publicly, have I been led to give a prophetic tongue. And I have never been used in giving a tongue as a miraculous sign gift, where it has manifested or been interpreted into a known language to unbelievers… yet. You see, these gifts are given by God, distributing them when and as He wills. Our prayer/praise language is the only variation that we can manifest at our discretion because it is *not* a manifestation "for the profit of all," but for a completely different purpose of self-edification.

Here is a breakdown of the different varieties of tongues:

Tongues for **Private Use**

Manifestation:	Personal Prayer/Spirit Language
Initiator:	Self
Recipient:	Self
Scripture Refs.:	1 Corinthians 13:1
	1 Corinthians 14:2,4,14-17
	Acts 2:1-12
	Acts 10:44-46
	Acts 19:1-7
	Ephesians 6:18
	Jude 20

Manifestation:	Intercession
Initiator:	Holy Spirit
Recipient:	Self / Others
	(Depending on for whom you're interceding)
Scripture Refs.:	1 Corinthians 13:1
	1 Corinthians 14:2, 14-15
	Romans 8:26-27

Tongues for **Public Ministry**

Manifestation:	Sign & Wonder
Initiator:	Holy Spirit
Recipient:	Others - Unbelievers
	(Hearers experiencing the miraculous by understanding or actual language)
Scripture Refs.:	1 Corinthians 13:1
	1 Corinthians 14:21-22
	Acts 2:1-12

Manifestation:	Prophetic Word
Initiator:	Holy Spirit
Recipient:	Others - Believers
	(Upon hearing the interpretation)
Scripture Refs.:	1 Corinthians 13:1
	1 Cor. 14:4-6, 13, 26-27

When you consider that there are different *varieties* of tongues, two for private use and two for public ministry, then it becomes more plausible that *some* tongues are for select people and *some* tongues can be for all. I will show you why this is true and provable using Paul's statement in 1 Corinthians 12:28-30.

> *And God has appointed these in the church: first apostles, second prophets, third teachers, after that miracles, then gifts of healings, helps, administrations, varieties of tongues.* 29 *Are all apostles? Are all prophets? Are all teachers? Are all workers of miracles?* 30 *Do all have gifts of healings? Do all speak with tongues? Do all interpret?* 1 Corinthians 12:28-30

So here, Paul is including three different classifications of gifts that are mentioned in other parts of Scripture:

> **Ascension Gifts (callings/roles)** - apostles, prophets, teachers.
>
> **Spiritual Gifts (supernatural)** - miracles, healings, *varieties* of tongues.
>
> **Motivational Gifts (natural)** – helps, administrations.

We could add more gifts to each of these classifications that are found throughout the New Testament, but it is not germane to my point.

Regarding the ascension gifts, are all saints called to have a specific appointed leadership role within the Church? No. So, if everyone is not called to be a teacher, then doesn't that exempt a portion of us who do not have that calling from discipling other people? Discipling people is *teaching* them about Jesus and God's Kingdom. Isn't making disciples of Christ part of His Great Commission to us all?

> *Go therefore and* ***make disciples*** *of all the nations, baptizing them in the name of the Father and of the Son and of the Holy Spirit...* Matthew 28:19

So, there is a difference between the public ministry and the role of a teacher in the Church and the act and responsibility of teaching. We could make the same correlation between an evangelist's calling versus our expected responsibility to evangelize. Are we all evangelists? No. Are we all expected to evangelize? No doubt. We could say the same about pastors. Are all called to be pastors? No. But if we are a parent, we are expected to shepherd, or pastor, the hearts and lives of our children (not to mention teaching). Additionally, whenever you disciple someone, you are, to some extent, shepherding them. It's just a matter of to what degree. Because you do not have a specific ***public*** role or calling that is recognized in the Church, it does not preclude you from performing some of those duties.

Then there are the supernatural spiritual gifts mentioned by Paul. Do all have gifts of healing? No. Do all have the ability to heal? As a disciple of Jesus, you bet! If you don't believe this, then your disagreement is with Jesus Himself. He says that it's a sign that is supposed to follow a believer in Mark 16:17-18:

> *And these signs will follow those who believe: In My name they will cast out demons; they will speak with new tongues; 18 they will take up serpents; and if they drink anything deadly, it will by no means hurt them;* ***they will lay hands on the sick, and they will recover****."* Mark 16:17-18

When Jesus first sent the Twelve out on their own, He commanded them *all* to heal the sick (Matthew 10:8). When He subsequently sent the Seventy out (Luke 10:9), He expected the same from *all* of them, not just the ones who had "the gift."

Since the principle of Paul's statement should apply to all the gifts, let's apply this to another spiritual gift... *the gift of faith.* 1 Corinthians 12:9 speaks of faith that's given to some people by the Spirit. So, using this same logic, does everybody have the gift of faith? No. Yet, "without faith, it is impossible to please God" (Hebrews 11:6). So, if you don't have the gift of faith, are you displeasing to God? We know that it is a *requirement* that every Christian has a measure of faith, or you are not even a Christian! So, it is possible to have faith, yet not have the "gift of faith". Thus, there is a subtle distinction between the different types of faith.

How about the gift of prophecy? To prophesy means either to *foretell* or to *forth-tell.* One function is to foretell something in the future; the other function is to discern and speak forth what the Holy Spirit is saying about any given thing or person in particular. Does everyone have the gift of prophecy? No. But can all prophesy? Yes. If you look at the *forth-telling* aspect of prophecy as just tuning in to the Lord and hearing what He is specifically saying about any given circumstance at the moment, then speaking it forth per His instruction, then you will be prophesying. This is just what an in-tune follower of Jesus Christ does as a Spirit-led son or daughter.

> *For as many as are led by the Spirit of God, these are sons of God.* Romans 8:14

The same differentiation applies to wisdom and knowledge (which we are instructed to obtain) and the spiritual gifts of "word of wisdom" and "word of knowledge". Another is discernment, versus the gift of "discerning of spirits". There are subtle differences and nuances within all of these. And so it is with speaking in varieties of tongues.

Regarding all the spiritual gifts, just because someone has operated in a specific power of a spiritual gift at one time, does not mean that they have the gift. I am aware that I have certain spiritual gifts. I know of them specifically because I see them operate in my life consistently, as well as operate at a higher level of power than somebody who does not have the gift. But, I also believe that I may operate in any of the gifts, at any time that God may need me or allow me to. That does not mean that I have that gift, per se. I know that I do not have the gift of interpretation of tongues. But that does not mean that I tune out or give up when I hear someone giving a prophetic tongue publicly in a service. I will always be asking the Lord if He needs or wants to use me for an interpretation. *I am always available*, not presuming that I am disqualified from serving or profiting from people in whichever way I am gifted or *not* gifted.

For example, at the time of this occurrence, I had not yet stepped into the gift of the *word of knowledge*. Yet, when my wife and I walked into a restaurant, I knew by my gift of *discerning of spirits* that a woman who worked there was a believer, as I sensed the Holy Spirit in her immediately upon seeing her. While we were eating, I asked God for a word for her to encourage and bless her. The Lord gave me a specific word of knowledge about her concern for a male family member who was in his early twenties, and that he was going to be okay. Before we left, I approached her and shared that I knew that she followed Jesus because I could sense Him in her, and then I shared the word of knowledge about the family member. Sure enough, there was an issue that was going on with her male, 24-year-old cousin for whom she was very concerned and had been praying. What I shared was a great blessing and encouragement to her. It was not my gift of the *word of knowledge* because I was not operating in that gift in my life at that time, but it was a moment when the Lord helped me to fulfill an opportunity for ministry to someone, by giving me a word of knowledge when the need arose. Do you see the difference?

Consider this. You are out at Walmart, and you see someone who is limping along with a hand holding her lower back in obvious pain. Compassion wells up from within you. You want to do something to help; you want to show the love of Jesus. If you have an incorrect understanding of these things that I am writing about in this chapter, then you will say to yourself, "I wish I could help her, but I don't have the gift of healing! If I could only get her to church on Sunday, where Bill, the bass guitar player on the worship team, could pray for her because Bill has the gift of healing." Sorry, but the Kingdom would never advance if that were the way that it worked. It is so important to expose these incorrect presumptions that we may have.

Now let's see how that same scenario plays out, considering what I have written as clarification to Paul's comments, and the subtle perfection that is found in operating in various spiritual gifts. Upon seeing the woman in pain, you realize that you are the only ambassador of the Kingdom of Heaven in this part of Walmart. If not you, then who? Additionally, you have been baptized in the Holy Spirit to be a witness of Jesus and to manifest His love for this woman in power and not just in words. Now, as far as you are concerned, you do not have the *gift of healing*, but you do know that one of the signs of a believer is healing. You approach the woman, step out in faith, and heal her back pain. You may not have as many healings as Bill, the bass guitar player at church, who does have the gift of healing, but you are obviously a disciple of Jesus Christ who was ready and able to pour out His love on a hurting world. "Well done, thy good and faithful servant! Because you have been faithful with few things, I will give you charge over many!"

In conclusion, there are two clarifying reasons that I could give for the "No" answer to Paul's question, "Do all speak with tongues?":

1) Well, to which tongues are you referring? Tongues for private prayer and spiritual self-strengthening, or for public ministry? Since these details were not the point that Paul was trying to make in the context of what he was addressing, he did not elaborate or make a distinction.

2) It is obvious that God wants *every Christian* to be baptized in (or filled with) the Holy Spirit with power. So, are all believers filled with the Holy Spirit?[3] No. So, why not? The answer is that there must first be a doctrinal belief in its validity as a starting point. Also, there must be a hunger and desire for it that outweighs

---

[3]There is a difference between the Holy Spirit within you as a result of salvation and being filled/baptized with the Holy Spirit. See my upcoming book, *Baptism of the Spirit & Fire*. Biblically, these are clearly two separate occurrences with different purposes.

fear, distrust, or any control issues regarding it. All do not speak in tongues because even those who have been ordained to speak in tongues as a public ministry must enter into it by faith, even after receiving the infilling of the Holy Spirit. It does not manifest itself automatically. Everyone must enter into all of the different types of tongues (as well as the other spiritual gifts) by faith. Because tongues are inarguably the most "foolish" of all of the spiritual gifts that challenge and short-circuit our human reasoning, it can be very daunting for some saints to enter into. It can be especially harder for those who are led by their intellect because tongues bypass human intellect by design.

Are all saved? No. Can they be? Yes. Do all believers speak in tongues? No. Can they? Yes, as their personal prayer/praise spirit language, but not necessarily as a public sign gift or as a prophetic gift. The former can be done at will, and the latter is dependent upon the Holy Spirit to initiate.

From Tower to Temple: The Prophetic Fulfillment of the Entire Church Speaking in Tongues

There is a difference between speaking in tongues as a public ministry gift and that of a spirit/prayer language. We must look at the overall meta-theme that the Lord is displaying for all of mankind to see as another witness to the fulfillment of His master plan. This is an amazing revelation that confirms how significant speaking in tongues is to the heart and plan of God, which is more than just a spiritual gift, *but is a prophetic sign and fulfillment in God's saga of Mankind.*

In Genesis 11:1-9, we read of the gathering of mankind on the plains of Shinar (or Babylon, modern-day Iraq):

> *Now the whole earth* ***had one language and one speech****.* [2] *And it came to pass, as they journeyed from the east, that they found a plain in the land of Shinar, and they dwelt there.* [3] *Then they said to one another, "Come, let us make bricks and bake them thoroughly." They had brick for stone, and they had asphalt for mortar.* [4] *And they said, "Come, let us build ourselves a city, and a tower whose top is in the heavens;* ***let us make a name for ourselves, lest we be scattered abroad*** *over the face of the whole earth."* [5] *But the LORD came down to see the city and the tower which the sons of men had built.* [6] *And the LORD said, "Indeed the people are one and they all have one language,* ***and this is what they begin to do****; now nothing that they propose to do will be withheld from them.* [7] *Come, let Us go down and there confuse their language, that they may not understand one another's speech."* [8] ***So the LORD scattered them abroad*** *from there over the face of all the earth, and they ceased building the city.* [9] *Therefore its name is called Babel, because there the LORD confused the language of all the earth; and from there the LORD scattered them abroad over the face of all the earth.* Genesis 11:1-9

We see in verse 4 that the motivation for building a city and a tower to the heavens was to *"make a name for ourselves, lest we be scattered abroad over the face of the earth."* Firstly, this was in direct contradiction to what God had commanded Noah and his sons to do after the flood, *"Be fruitful and multiply and fill the earth"* (Genesis 9:1). But more so, it seems that they desired to build a monument (the Tower of Babel) to themselves that attested to their greatness, reaching the heavens. We can assume that this misdirected cooperation among the sons of men, fueled by selfish pride, would have resulted in more of the same wickedness that prompted the Lord to bring on the judgment of the Great Flood, in Genesis 6, previously. When the Lord confused their languages, this caused divisions amongst the people so that they could not work together. Consequently, the building of the city and tower stopped, and the people were scattered abroad over the face of the earth, according to God's previous instruction.

Conversely, on the Day of Pentecost, in Jerusalem, when Jews from the various tribes and tongues of people who were *"from every nation under heaven"* (Acts 2:1-12) were gathered together, God, the Holy Spirit, came down again to reverse the curse of confusion by bestowing one language; the language of the Spirit. The language of the Spirit, or tongues, was a prophetic sign that declared the glory and praises of God that were interpreted (in their hearing) into every tongue of every nation, as a witness that something new and earth-shaking was happening—the birth of the Church—through which the Gospel was to be preached throughout the earth. This was a re-establishment of God's original intent for Mankind and the earth, starting with Adam and Eve, to be a united family with our Creator Father, with the curse and burden of sin lifted!

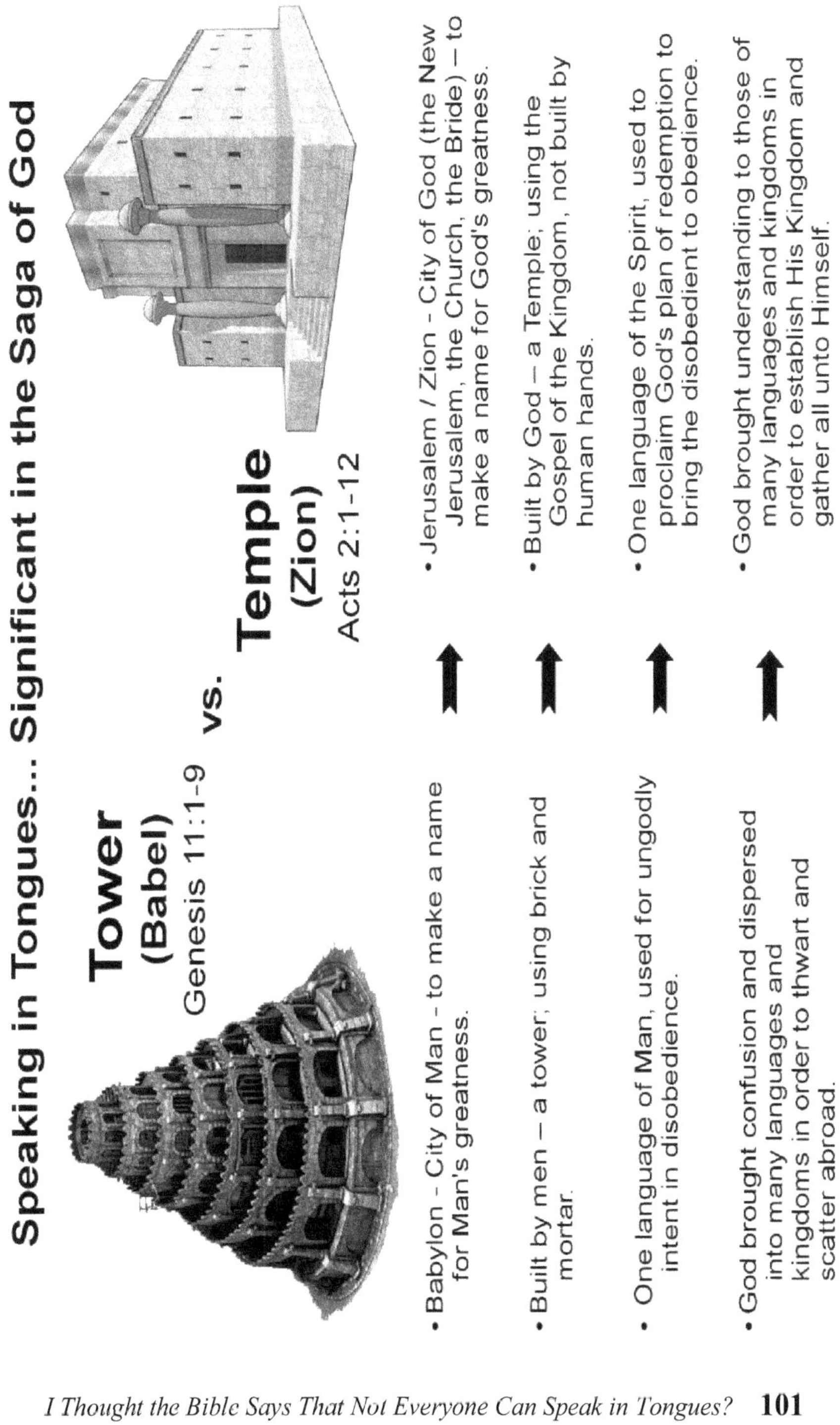
Speaking in Tongues… Significant in the Saga of God
Tower
(Babel)
Genesis 11:1-9
vs.
Temple
(Zion)
Acts 2:1-12
• Babylon - City of Man - to make a name for Man's greatness.
• Jerusalem / Zion - City of God (the New Jerusalem, the Church, the Bride) – to make a name for God's greatness.
• Built by men – a tower; using brick and mortar.
• Built by God – a Temple; using the Gospel of the Kingdom, not built by human hands.
• One language of Man, used for ungodly intent in disobedience.
• One language of the Spirit, used to proclaim God's plan of redemption to bring the disobedient to obedience.
• God brought confusion and dispersed into many languages and kingdoms in order to thwart and scatter abroad.
• God brought understanding to those of many languages and kingdoms in order to establish His Kingdom and gather all unto Himself.

So, as you can see, there is much more to tongues than just being one of the nine spiritual gifts. It was given to every person upon receiving the baptism of the Holy Spirit as a prophetic sign of something greater in God's interaction with Mankind.

Spiritual Elitism?

From my experience, virtually everyone who does speak in tongues believes and teaches that *all believers* can speak in tongues as a private prayer/praise spirit language if they receive the baptism of the Holy Spirit and are open to stepping into it. This fact contradicts some people's faulty objections that would sound like, "Well, you guys who pray in tongues think that you're better than people who don't! You think that you're more spiritual than everyone else!" Well, let's answer both of those deflective decoys with simple logic.

Firstly, if someone in any social dynamic has an "elitist attitude" when comparing themselves with others, they typically **always want to bar the access** of those who are "inferior", from attaining the "superior/elite" status that they have attained, thus maintaining their presumed status of superiority. This is exemplified by how:

- "Old money" looks down on "new money".
- Nobility/aristocracy looks down on the peasantry.
- White-collar people can look down on blue-collar.
- Officers can look down on enlisted men.

Fortunately, this is exactly the opposite of what I have seen displayed and proclaimed by saints who speak in tongues. They have a deep desire for *every* follower of Jesus to enter into the blessedness of being able to share in the deep spiritual expression of their love and affection for their Savior. They also want all to have access to God's weight room, where they can build up their most holy faith, bypassing the limitations of their human understanding. Freely they have received, freely they want to give. The people who pray in tongues are *never* the ones actively limiting others from doing the same… it just doesn't happen. The obstacles that are placed in the way of people receiving tongues are, however, always put there by the people themselves or their teachers, who also do not exercise the ability. That may be hard to hear, but it is true. Who is limiting you from entering into receiving this ability? It's probably your theological upbringing and understanding, **not** those who speak in tongues themselves. Heck, we want you to join in and see what you've been missing… for Jesus' sake!

Secondly, concerning being more spiritual, not more mature (sanctification), but more spiritual (empowered). Some very spiritually astute people are immature in character.

Very simply, imagine that you have two football players who are equally talented and committed, who are competing against each other for just one open starting position on the first string. One of those players works out and lifts in the weight room five days a week, and the other player doesn't hit the weights at all. Who do you think is going to be the stronger player? That strength will make a difference on the field, in the game, where it counts. It's safe to say that the starter will be the one who availed himself to make use of the tools that were afforded to him to get stronger. It was a matter of choice and effort, not a disparity of opportunity.

Does God Give Some an Unfair Advantage?

Since we know that "God is no respecter of persons" (Acts 10:34), imagine if there were a disparity of opportunity. One player had a key to the weight room, where he could build up his muscles day after day, week after week, and month after month. The other player was denied access to that same weight room just because the coach wanted to give the key to one player and not the other. In the natural, this makes no sense for a coach to do this. ***He wants all his players to be as individually strong as possible***, no matter what position they play. In the same way, as discussed in an earlier chapter, if speaking in tongues as a prayer language, is the ***only spiritual gift that is used for self-edification***, that builds a believer up in their inner spirit-man, then it would make no sense for the Lord to give the gift of tongues for private, personal use to one of His children, yet deny that same strengthening opportunity to another.

Do you think that God decides to give a Bible to one believer for His strengthening, yet denies another the same text? Yet, a person born in America will have ample opportunity to access the Word of God for his/her personal strengthening, while a person born in Saudi Arabia will not have that opportunity. So, in a situation like this, we obviously say that that is NOT the will of God. We believe that He wants the Saudis to have the same opportunity to access the Word of Life as He wants for the Americans. So, wouldn't we smuggle Bibles into a nation like Saudi Arabia to rectify that disparity? But similarly, we sit by and make the same discrimination between fellow believers by using a theological argument that says one person has access to this gift of personal strengthening by the Spirit, and another does not, simply by the sovereign choosing of God. It's nonsense and illogical, as well as not supported by all of the other, real-life examples found in Scripture, as you will see.

If You're Going to Gamble, Play the Odds

If you are going to double down on your doctrinal belief that not all Christians can speak in tongues, wouldn't it be wise to consider what the odds are before you place your bet? What are the numbers, statistically speaking, that would convince you to wager something as valuable as a gift from and an ability to connect to your Heavenly Father?

In the Bible, I estimate that thousands of people received the baptism of the Holy Spirit. However, the specific first-hand accounts (of which there are three) total approximately 150-200+ people. In our attempt to have our Christian experience line up with the Scriptures, let's take a look at those accounts, and more specifically, regarding speaking in tongues:

- <u>Acts 2:1-5</u>

  120 disciples in the upper room on the Day of Pentecost. Of the 120 who were filled, how many spoke in tongues? *All* 120 of them.
  120 of 120 = 100%

- <u>Acts 10:44-46</u>

  20-100 (a reasonable estimate) of the household of Cornelius, the centurion; his family, friends, and servants. Of these people, *all* spoke in tongues upon receiving the baptism of the Holy Spirit.
  20-100 of 20-100 = 100%

- <u>Acts 19:1-7</u>

  12 Ephesian disciples who had believed but had not been water baptized, nor had received the BOTHS yet. When Paul laid hands upon them, *all* twelve began to speak in tongues and magnify God.
  12 of 12 = 100%

If you must place a bet on this (which you are whether you realize it or not), do you not think that it is significant that in the Book of Acts, of all the first-hand accounts of believers receiving the baptism of the Holy Spirit, 100% of them spoke in tongues?

Additionally, we know that when the Apostle Paul was prayed for by Ananias of Damascus, and the scales fell from Paul's eyes, he was also baptized in the Holy Spirit:

> *"Brother Saul, the Lord Jesus, who appeared to you on the road as you came, has sent me that you may receive your sight **and be filled with the Holy Spirit**."* Acts 9:17

So, from Paul's own words in 1 Corinthians 14:18, *"I thank my God I speak with tongues more than you all..."*, shows us that he did also. **1 of 1 = 100%.**

Which is feeling like a safer doctrinal wager? Play the odds, and it will pay off very well.

When Personal Experience & Scriptural Examples Align

I believe that I have established several biblical pieces of evidence that warrant "reasonable doubt" regarding the supposition that every Spirit-filled believer cannot speak or pray in tongues. Now, I can submit to you my own experience getting people baptized in the Holy Spirit, and the results that are in alignment with my stated beliefs, as well as these scriptural examples that were 100% consistent.

Receiving the baptism of the Holy Spirit was a life-altering event in my Christian walk. Since then, I have laid hands on hundreds of Christians worldwide who have then had the power of God come upon them, as they were filled with the Holy Spirit. Every single one of them, who were baptized with the Holy Spirit and stepped out in faith, has spoken in tongues—100%.

For some, it immediately came like a flood out of them. For others, they needed a little help and encouragement to "let go" and trust God, turning their human reasoning off. They needed to be encouraged to jump into the flow of the River of Life that they were experiencing, where they began to flow with what God was doing in them, jumping into the flow of the Spirit.

Some tip-toed cautiously in, as if not wanting to get wet. But, because I know that God wants everyone to be able to "pray in the Spirit, building up your most holy faith", I would not let them go until they were flowing in their own, new spirit language.

It is such a vital tool for the Spirit-empowered life. Everyone with whom I stuck it out, making them comfortable with their new spirit-to-Spirit communication with the Lord, has been very grateful afterward. Because I understand the obstacles that well-intended, yet destructively incorrect teaching has done to hinder God's people from receiving His very best, I persevere with everyone in this way.

It's very significant to point out that in *all* my aforementioned experiences, the Christians who have come from a background that has taught negatively on tongues, or the things of the Spirit, have the most difficulty entering into tongues. People who are simply hungry for God, are new believers, or are just ignorant that there's even such a thing as speaking in tongues, enter into it quite easily, once told what God wants to give to them.

Keep in mind that each of us will still need to give an account to the Lord for all of the spiritual fruit and works that He has ordained for us to produce, according to the graces made available to us, regardless of whether we have discovered them or not.

It is wiser to err on the side of faith and hunger for more than to prematurely exempt yourself from receiving something from God due to fear, unbelief, or uncomfortability. *If He has designated that you are not to have the gift of tongues,* ***then ask Him to tell you that unequivocally****!* Ask Him from a sincere heart, rather than preemptively deciding upon it based on your limited understanding. I think that is a fair-minded request, and well-pleasing to God.

Chapter Seven

"Why Do We Need Tongues When We Have the Bible?"

In Spirit AND Truth

"But the hour is coming, and now is, when the true worshipers will worship the Father in *spirit* and *truth*; for the Father is seeking such to worship Him. God is Spirit, and those who worship Him ***must*** worship in spirit and truth." John 4:23-24

Notice that Jesus said, "must". It is a great folly to dismiss and overlook that one word. Allow me to expound.

The "sword of the Spirit" is the Word of God (Ephesians 6:17)—the Truth. Jesus Christ is "the Word that became flesh" (John 1:14), and "the living Word" (Hebrews 4:12). Jesus said of Himself, "I am the way, *the truth*, and the life..." So, Jesus is the living Word of God, the Truth. That is why in the book of Revelation, a two-edged sword proceeds out of His mouth.

Everything He is, says, and does is Truth, the Word, the "sword of the spirit".

The Bible is not just an ideological set of principles for living life, but it claims to be supernatural; "spirit and life" (John 6:63). It is not a book *about* truth. It is an autobiography *of* Truth. Truth is not a "what", it is a "Who".

However, having the Word, or truth, is not enough. The Pharisees & Sadducees had the Word. But because they viewed, understood, and practiced the perfect Law, by the soul of Man (human reasoning and the wisdom of Man), they ended up making the Word of no effect and perverting the spirit, heart, and purpose behind the Word. The wrong spirit behind the Word will make the truth no longer the Truth.

If God planned to just give us a set of rules to follow and obey, then He would have stopped at the Law of Moses, and/or Jesus would have miraculously left us a completed New Testament to follow before He left, just as Joseph Smith had written the Book of Mormon for the Mormons, or Mohamed had written the Qur'an for his Muslim followers.

No, if the Father's endgame was just to set up Jesus as the earthly King for all to love, honor, and obey His decrees, then He would not have taken Him to Heaven and sent the Holy Spirit to us. God's eternal purpose was to dwell not only among His people but as one *in* His people; complete *oneness* with Him, by His Spirit.

When we, as the Church, neglect the reality of the presence of the Spirit of the Lord not only in our doctrinal views, but in our church services, our day-to-day living, and in our idea of what basic fundamental Christianity is, then we thwart the very heart of God's eternal purpose. Christianity then becomes just another ideology in the marketplace of world religions. Without Christians having the *manifested* presence of God in our lives and in our gatherings, we are reduced to offering the world the very same thing as all of the other world religions: self-help principles and a set of rules and standards by which one can have clean living and a higher set moral compass. This reduces the Bible to the same equivalency as other "holy" books, like the Qur'an, Book of Mormon, Hindu Vedas, Buddhist Tripitaka, etc. And this is *not* biblical Christianity.

Conversely, having the Holy Spirit alone is not enough. Even though we are promised by Jesus that "the Spirit of Truth will guide you into all truth" (John 16:13*), the shortcoming is not with the Holy Spirit;* ***it is with us***. The Spirit can and will do this, but can we always hear Him? If we do hear Him, do we recognize that it is Him and not ourselves? And if we do hear Him clearly, will we listen and obey?

The connection and relation between the soul and the spirit can be quite complicated and convoluted for us. To clarify this for us (what is Him, what is us), God has given us His Word to help give us a foundational baseline from which to measure and process all of our experiences. He tells us stories to show us how and what He thinks in various life situations—this is one of the primary ways by which we learn how to know His character and His ways. The Scriptures help to teach us to know Him and ourselves. They are the launching pad, guardrail, and measuring stick for all of our life-in-the-spirit with Him.

The Spirit and the Truth are really one and the same. They do not contradict one another because they are the same Person. In the Scriptures, the Holy Spirit is called "the Spirit of Truth" and "the Spirit of Christ". So it is impossible to separate the Holy Spirit from Jesus (the Word of God), without falling into error. Whenever we separate them or detract from, or honor one ***at the expense of the other***, we make it/Him of no effect and miss the heart, spirit, and purpose of what He is saying. *And then it is no longer truth.*

According to Jesus' words in John 4:23-24, God is seeking those who will worship Him and walk in the fullness of ***both*** the Spirit and the Truth. He states that a "true worshiper" ***must do both***. Once the Church at large gets this revelation, we will become the Bride that is ready for her Bridegroom, without spot or wrinkle, and all of Creation will see the "manifestation of the Sons of God" for which it is groaning.

Regarding worshipping in Spirit and in Truth, the sword of the Spirit is the Word/Truth. The Spirit is the Holy Spirit-filled and led heart (hand) that enables the Word (sword) to be wielded as God intended.

If our heart is not established in truth…

> *"The heart is deceitful above all things and desperately wicked; Who can know it?"* Jeremiah 17:9

> *"Behold, You (GOD) desire truth in the inward parts (of us)…"* Psalm 51:6 *(parentheses added)*

If the spirit by which we read the Word is based on human, natural understanding…

> *"But the natural man does not receive the things of the Spirit of God, for they are foolishness to him; nor can he know them, because they are spiritually discerned."* 1 Corinthians 2:14

…then, we will misuse (probably unintentionally) the Word for harm, exactly the opposite of its intended purpose. But *the* most frightening reality is that we will be deceived into thinking that we are *defending* the truth from elements of deception:

> *" ...yes, the time is coming that whoever kills you will think that he offers God service."* John 16:2

We *must* have the utmost fear of the Lord when dealing with the sharpest object in the history of the universe, and be committed to not trusting and leaning on our own understanding when handling it.

The Bible: A Book of Mysteries

> *It is the glory of God to conceal a matter, but the glory of kings is to search out a matter.* Proverbs 25:2

> *And sitting in his chariot(an Ethiopian eunuch), he was reading Isaiah the prophet. Then the Spirit said to Philip, "Go near and overtake this chariot." So Philip ran to him, and heard him reading the prophet Isaiah, and said, "Do you understand what you are reading?" And he said, "How can I, unless someone guides me?"* Acts 8:28-31

Reading the Gospels, you will see that a majority of what Jesus taught was on the "mysteries" or spiritual truths of God and His Kingdom. Jesus even told His disciples,

> *"To you it has been given to know the mysteries (or hidden truths) of the kingdom of God, but to the rest it is given in parables..." Luke 8:10*

The Apostle Paul states,

> *"Let a man so consider us, as servants of Christ and stewards of the mysteries of God." 1 Corinthians 4:1*

Additionally,

> *"But God has revealed them (the mysteries) to us through His Spirit. For the Spirit searches all things, yes, the deep things of God. 1 Corinthians 2:10*

Other than Jesus Christ himself, what man (that we know of) had the most revelation of the Lord's spiritual truths? I believe that most would agree that it was the Apostle Paul. From Paul, we have over half of the New Testament and some of the most consequential, foundational Church doctrines and understanding of the details of what a life in Christ means. All of this is from a man who never once met Jesus while He was alive as a man. That is some serious revelation. This is the kind of person that, if we were smart, would go and ask him, "How did you get such amazing revelations about these things, and how do I get them as well?"

Well, he gives us a hint in 1 Corinthians 14:8, *"I thank my God I speak with tongues more than you all..."*. If when you pray in tongues, you pray out the mysteries of God, does it not make sense that you will have a greater understanding (revelation) of those mysteries (truths) the more that you pray in tongues? Although Paul was brilliant intellectually, he never once credited his revelations to his intellect or religious training. Christianity is not an intellectual pursuit. It is a desire for, and openness to, Spirit and Truth. Thus, there are no natural barriers to spiritual growth, maturity, and understanding, making it available to "whosoever will". Jesus said,

> *"I praise you, Father, Lord of heaven and earth, because you have hidden these things from the wise and learned, and revealed them to little children." Matthew 11:25*

Becoming Foolish to Become Wise

> *For he who speaks in a tongue does not speak to men but to God, for no one understands him; however, in the spirit he speaks mysteries. (v. 2)*

> *For if I pray in a tongue, my spirit prays, but my understanding is unfruitful*. (v. 14)

At first glance, verse 14 sounds like a drawback, but it is absolutely my favorite benefit! When Paul says, *"My understanding is unfruitful"*, he is referring to his mind. So, in other words, Paul is saying that when he prays in tongues, his mind does not understand what he is saying. How could this be beneficial? So, to understand this, let us first look at what the Bible says about our own human wisdom, understanding, and reasoning:

> *Trust in the Lord with all your heart, and lean not on your own understanding*... Proverbs 3:5

> *"For My thoughts are not your thoughts, nor are your ways My ways," says the LORD. "For as the heavens are higher than the earth, so are My ways higher than your ways, and My thoughts than your thoughts*. Isaiah 55:8-9

> *(The Lord) ...who turns wise men backward, and makes their knowledge foolishness*... Isaiah 44:25

The mind governed by the flesh is hostile to God; it does not submit to God's law, nor can it do so. Romans 8:7 *NIV*

Because the foolishness of God is wiser than men, and the weakness of God is stronger than men.
1 Corinthians 1:25

But God has chosen the foolish things of the world to put to shame the wise... 1 Corinthians 1:27

These things we also speak, not in words which man's wisdom teaches but which the Holy Spirit teaches, comparing spiritual things with spiritual. But the natural man does not receive the things of the Spirit of God, for they are foolishness to him; nor can he know them, because they are spiritually discerned.
1 Corinthians 2:13-14

And my speech and my preaching were not with persuasive words of human wisdom, but in demonstration of the Spirit and of power, that your faith should not be in the wisdom of men but in the power of God. 1 Corinthians 2:4-5

For the wisdom of this world is foolishness with God. For it is written, "He catches the wise in their own craftiness"... 1 Corinthians 3:9

There is a way that seems right to a man, but its end is the way of death. Proverbs 16:5

Although God does not expect, nor want us to "check our brains at the door," the biblical view of Man's mind—our human understanding and reasoning—is *not at all* flattering.

So much of what the Lord wants to show us and do through us is thwarted by our need to apply our own natural thoughts, opinions, religious training, and understanding to Kingdom truths that are spiritual in nature.

> *"But the natural man does not receive the things of the Spirit of God, for they are foolishness to him, nor can he know them..."* 1 Cor. 2:14

Thus, we are admonished by Jesus Himself that if we do not "become like a child," we will not even enter the Kingdom of God. So, did He mean that we are required to act silly and immature, quitting our jobs and shirking our responsibilities so that we can just play and have fun all the time? I wish. But no, the key intention of what Jesus meant is summed up in one word: *teachable.*

Since God "knows our frame" (Ps. 103:14), He understands that our default mode is to trust in what we already know, through intellect and experience. Thus, it is very difficult for us to believe in and trust in that which we do not yet know. This is why faith is so important to God. "But, without faith, it is impossible to please Him." (Hebrews 11:6).

Therefore, knowing our weakness and tendencies, He has given us a gift and tool that enables us to strengthen our spirit-man while bypassing our human understanding, which limits us from entering the fullness of the Spirit because of unbelief. I discuss this in greater detail, as well as the findings of a medical study that was done on brain activity while speaking in tongues, in chapter 7, *Spirit Muscle.*

Many times, in life, we are faced with a situation or a decision where we are not exactly sure how to respond. To better decide, we usually fall back on the biblical principles that we have learned from our Bible knowledge, presuming that God would want us to respond accordingly. The only problem is that this assumes that our initial biblical knowledge is complete and not flawed.

An example of this is in Luke 9, when two of Jesus' disciples, the brothers James and John, came to a Samaritan village that they were to prepare for Jesus' arrival. The village rejected the offer. When they heard the village's rejection, they went to Jesus and presumed that He wanted them to do the biblical thing, according to their knowledge and understanding—"Lord, do You want us to command fire to come down from heaven and consume them, just as Elijah did?" Well, after all, it's scriptural, isn't it? 2 Kings, chapter 1—call down fire from heaven and then kill all of those who will not receive and submit to the Lord's ways. In their minds, this seemed perfectly in line with what the Bible says about what God would want them to do. A little fire and brimstone upon the faithless heathens who do not want to turn from their wicked ways, ala Sodom and Gomorrah?

But let's see how Jesus reacted to this:

> *But He turned and rebuked them, and said, "You do not know* <u>*what manner of spirit*</u> *you are of. For the Son of Man did not come to destroy men's lives but to save them." And they went to another village.* Luke 9:55-56

So, these two were not even in the same ballpark as God. I bet just before they approached Jesus with the news, they might have felt like they were going to get some extra brownie points with the Messiah for throwing in a little biblical insight to show that they had been paying attention in synagogue all of those years. But, before we are too hard on the boys, realize that we do the same thing… constantly. Only, it's just not recorded for posterity to see.

As a matter of fact, we should neither sanctimoniously point the finger at the Pharisees, Sadducees, or teachers of the Law, either, as we are one faulty doctrine away from acting just like them. We should not mentally berate the typical Jews of Jesus' day for not signing up in masse for a round of suffering to follow this revolutionary boat-rocker, of whom half the people claimed was a prophet, and the other half claimed was a demonized charlatan. We can lack the same discernment and be just as coerced to "tow the party line" by our own fear of rejection and peer pressure as well. When we read about the ancient Israelites throughout the Old Testament, or the religious people of Jesus' day, we should not slap our palms to our foreheads and exclaim, "How could they be so stupid and go astray from the Lord, yet again?" For our hearts can go astray as easily as theirs did.

In addition, how many different interpretations of Scripture do we have? If we are relying on our human intellect and understanding, then we can, will, and do come up with many varied interpretations of just one verse, let alone the major themes of Scripture.

So, because we have all these glaring deficiencies in our nature which God so repeatedly points out, and because we have seen through the entire meta-narrative of the Bible of how men can corrupt that which is pure, lovely, and perfect… we need God. No, not in a rhetorical, lip-servicing way, but we actually must learn and digest the truth, by the Spirit of Truth. It is the difference between reading a biography ***of*** a person written by someone else, or an autobiography written ***by*** the very person. Who better to understand what the author of a story meant than the author Himself?

As mentioned in Chapter 3, when we pray in tongues, we pray out mysteries, spirit to Spirit, directly to God—our words empowered and directed by the Holy Spirit Himself. When people realize that getting to know the Author of the Book is of equal importance as knowing the Book, then we can better interpret what He meant in the Book.

When we come upon a verse where we have no idea what was meant by it or there may even be several obvious possible interpretations; instead of reaching to a bookshelf for our trusty commentary (which is just another man's opinion), why don't we stop and ask God what He meant when He had that verse written? Then, pray in the Spirit, all the while knowing that we and He are communicating on a higher level, bypassing our unfruitful human mind but praying out mysteries in the Spirit. In faith, we trust that He is spiritually downloading the answers to these mysteries to us as we surrender our tongue and sometimes our embarrassment and personal sense of dignity, to pray them out.

When there is a verse or concept that we are reading and we can sense that there is much more buried in those verses or comments that Jesus made... pray in tongues, believing that we are praying what is currently hidden and unknown to us, into our understanding.

Think of it this way, you are a treasure hunter headed out to a local beach. You plan to scour the sand with your metal detector to find a hidden treasure: coins, watches, jewelry, etc. In this case, the revelations of the spiritual mysteries of the Kingdom are the hidden treasures buried underneath the sands of your lack of understanding. The metal detector is speaking in tongues, which detects (or connects with) those treasures that your natural eyes (mind) cannot see.

Knowing the Beginning from the End

Another aspect of praying out the mysteries of God entails that which the future holds for us, our families, and friends. Since we do not know the future, we do not know specifically what we need to pray for, or against. But the Lord does:

> *...I am God, and there is none like Me, declaring the end from the beginning, and from ancient times things that are not yet done, saying, 'My counsel shall stand, and I will do all My pleasure"...* Isaiah 46:9-10

With tongues, in faith, by the Spirit, we can pray out this counsel from the Lord. I know that by His grace, He has us pray for things that are headed our way about which we are clueless. And, if He told us the details, we would probably mess it up with our worrying or manipulating it to try and avoid or to improve upon it. Jesus said, "Each day has enough trouble of its own." Matt. 6:34 *NKJV*

When I was an inner-city missionary, I was spending time with the Lord and praying in tongues. Because I know that when you pray in tongues, you are praying out the mysteries of God, but your mind does not know what you are praying, I am always aware that God can drop understanding from my spirit into my mind as I am praying. As I was praying in tongues, the thought came into my mind, "Make me the calm in the storm, make me the eye of the storm." Because I sensed that that was from the Holy Spirit, I prayed it out in English. I then returned to tongues, noting this as something significant, but not understanding its usefulness or application.

A couple of days later, as I was in the backyard of the men's ministry house, talking to one of the young men. We heard a very loud screeching of brakes and a loud thud from the street in front of the house. We ran around the front of the house, where we saw a man lying out in the middle of the street about fifty feet away from the front of a pickup truck that had just struck and thrown him.

I immediately sprang into action, giving directions to my friend to call 911, and then running out into the street to see the man. He was an elderly Hispanic man in his late seventies to early eighties, and he was lying on his side, still conscious, not able to talk, and bleeding out of his ears. I immediately knew that this was a life-or-death situation and that any fear or apprehension on my part was not going to serve this man well.

I began to yell out prayers in English, declaring life over him, forbidding a spirit of death from coming upon him. I began telling him in Spanish, "¡Llame a Jesús Cristo!", meaning "Call out to Jesus Christ!" I was yelling in tongues over him, interceding, as well. This was a poor neighborhood, so there were always people walking on the streets. Through this, I noticed about three or four people who were standing near us, about eight feet away, and they looked panic-stricken and too scared to even come near the man, let alone to do anything to help. For that split second, the fear of man and my human reasoning kicked in, and I wondered what these people must be thinking of me right now. But it was only a fleeting thought as I calmly and confidently, but very actively, stood in the gap for this man's life and even maybe his eternal soul. The calm that had come over me to act was otherworldly.

Eventually, the paramedics arrived and took him. There was a couple in the truck, and the man driving had been drinking heavily and did not see the elderly man. I was told that he was trying to get his wife to say that she was driving, so as not to get arrested. I do not know what became of the situation, of either the driver or the victim. I do not know whether he lived or died.

But what I do know is that the man who was struck was probably someone's husband, father, grandfather, brother, or uncle. And if those were his final moments on earth, I wanted those family members to know that he was not alone, that there was someone there who cared more about him, a stranger, than he cared about what people thought about the crazy antics that were employed to battle for his life and soul. I wonder if he called out to the Savior in his heart as he was looking at me, knowing it was a very bad situation. I wanted the family to know that God so loved this man that He had prepared someone spiritually, just days before, to be the one who was present at their beloved father's side during his greatest time of need.

In my life, I have been present for some similar traumatic crises in people's lives. Typically, incredible exhaustion, both emotional and physical, hits you after the crisis has wound down. After this encounter, I did not experience any of that. It was so evident to me throughout the entire incident that I was the calm in that storm, knowing exactly what had to be done and doing it in a way that was urgent and forceful, yet assuring.

Now, when praying in tongues, I am always aware that the Lord may give me a word of understanding as to what mysteries that I may be praying out. Thus, I can agree in my mind as well as with my mouth, by praying in English. Nonetheless, if He does not give me understanding, it is no less preparing me for what may be coming than if I did pray it in English. He is still aligning my spirit and preparing me, regardless. I am so grateful for this gift and that He understands what we need, far more than we do.

Beyond Our Ability

Here are two other examples of how tongues were used to pray for needs that I was completely unaware of, but I was spiritually available for the Lord to use me in the respective situations, regardless of how it looked.

The first was when I was praying with a group of elders from the church that I was attending. As we were all waiting upon the Lord, I felt the Holy Spirit rising up within my spirit and that He wanted me to begin interceding in tongues, beyond my typical personal prayer language. Now, almost all of us were praying in tongues individually off-and-on, but this was a sense of Him wanting to do something on a different level. As I began to pray in the Spirit out loud, it became more and more forceful as the presence of the Lord came upon me in greater and greater waves. The language definitely sounded like an Asian language, but whether it was an actual or spiritual language, we did not know, but it was with such intensity that all knew that it was something that God was behind.

This must have continued for at least 20 minutes, everyone being still or praying in tongues individually, being sensitive to the Lord for their part, while I made whatever declarations I was making in the Spirit. As the Spirit lifted off of me, one of the men said that I was interceding, at that very moment, for the very life of a persecuted believer in China and told us what his name was. Well, we will only know for certain the details on the other side of eternity. But I am grateful to those spiritual men for keeping watch on the wall with me and not being negligent in their spiritual gifts and prayer language.

The second incident was after we had held a mid-week service at our local church. Where I live, in Southern California, we have many First Nations tribal reservations. There was a group of four First Nations brothers and sisters whom I did not know, who had stopped by our service and were hanging out afterward.

There were probably twelve people left in the sanctuary, and I had entered the raised platform sound booth that was in the back of the sanctuary to power down all of the sound equipment. As I was standing in the booth, one of my congregants standing with the group yelled to me that this group was heading out to China in a couple of days. As soon as I heard this, the Spirit of the Lord fell upon me, and the weightiness of it caused me to double over, holding onto the soundboard. Tongues began flowing out of my spirit and mouth. It was so sudden and uninhibited that everyone turned to look and see what had just happened.

Since I have learned to completely surrender myself, in cooperation, to the Holy Spirit when I feel His unction, I was able to flow with whatever He was doing, and I was not about to stop it because I understand that it is *for* something—a purpose in the spirit realm. The interesting and challenging thing was this: I sounded like a munchkin from *The Wizard of Oz*… you know, "Follow the yellow brick road!" But it was all in an Asian-sounding language similar to Chinese or Vietnamese.

Well, there were roars of laughter at the loss of all my pastoral dignity (which is way overrated anyway), and at the sound of a Chinese/Vietnamese munchkin yelling from the floor of the sound booth. The floor, because by this time I was on my hands and knees under the counter that the soundboard was on, as waves of intercession rolled over me. Luckily, all of these people were familiar with manifestations such as this because they were familiar with the Holy Spirit moving in power upon the saints.

Admittedly, to my mind, I knew that this sounded hilarious and ridiculous... but I was not laughing. I was sweating and praying... hard. I sensed that an angel was standing behind me, and as I would intercede aggressively, non-stop, for 20-30 seconds at a time, I would get physically winded, and then I would feel the glory lift off me for about 10 seconds until I caught my breath again. Then, it was as if the angel would lay his hand on my head again, and a wave of God's Spirit would come upon me again, and it would ramp right back up to top speed again for another 20-30 seconds.

Each new successive wave of prayer would result in a wave of laughter from the others. Then, sometime in the middle of it all, I began singing in this childlike, Asian voice. Even more laughter. After about five solid minutes of this, the waves of unction began to subside, and I no longer felt the angelic presence behind me. I was left on my knees on the floor of the sound booth, under the soundboard, panting and sweating, but knowing that God had just done something powerful through me, but not very dignifying by human reasoning.

As I pulled myself up to my feet, everyone was looking at me, curious to see what the heck had happened to me. I could only say, "Wow!" Then one of the First Nations women said, "Do you know what we are going to do in China? We are going to minister to little children in schools all over China!"

So, to the best that we could decipher, having Chinese children sing praises to Jesus was on God's agenda, and He wanted me to make sure that it was declared and that any obstacles to that occurring were torn down in the spirit realm first, before this team went out to do it. No planning or discussion could have orchestrated that happening in such a powerful, sovereign way. And if I knew the details of what I was going to do beforehand, I probably would not have volunteered. But, years ago, when I first got baptized in the Holy Spirit, I said, "Yes!" to God for whatever He needed of me. I urge you to do the same, and speaking in tongues is a big part of it.

> *"Do you hear what these children are saying?" they asked him. "Yes," replied Jesus, "have you never read, "'From the lips of children and infants you, Lord, have called forth your praise'?"* Matthew 21:16 *NIV*

Chapter Eight

Spirit Muscle: "How Can I Better Tune in to the Holy Spirit, Flow in My Spiritual Gifts, and Build Spirit Muscle?"

Soul vs. Spirit

As I stated earlier, I believe that one of the greatest deficiencies in the Body of Christ is a lack of familiarity with and empowerment of the Holy Spirit. One of the main consequences of this deficiency is the inability of many, if not most Christians, to recognize the difference between that which is soulish and that which is Spirit. The Bible states that there is a difference:

> *Now may the God of peace Himself sanctify you completely; and may your whole spirit, soul, and body be preserved blameless at the coming of our Lord Jesus Christ.* Thessalonians 5:23

> *For the word of God is living and powerful, and sharper than any two-edged sword, piercing even to* ***the division of soul and spirit****...* Hebrews 4:12

So not only does the appropriate application of the Word of God enable us to recognize the difference between soul and spirit, but also does walking in familiarity and intimacy with the Holy Spirit. We can spend time "in the spirit" as the Bible speaks of, praying and worshipping in tongues.

Upon receiving the baptism of the Holy Spirit, *every believer* can develop their spiritual senses to be able to discern whether something that is happening is coming from the Holy Spirit, a demonic spirit, or more often, the soul realm of Man. There is also a specific spiritual gift that enables us to recognize this at a more consistent and higher level—the gift of *discerning of spirits* (1 Corinthians 12:10).

There is a significant difference between ministry that is of the Spirit and ministry that is from the soul. For many people who have not been baptized in the Holy Spirit, soulish things are often believed to be of the Spirit of God but are not. They are from the hearts and minds of men, but sound good and are often correct.

Before we are born-again through faith in Jesus Christ, our spirit, our very life essence, is dead to God. We are alive as spirit beings, but we are dead in our sins. Before we get saved by the blood of Jesus as payment for our sins, we truly are "the walking dead" by God's standards. That is why Jesus said that we *must* be born again to enter God's Kingdom.

When we are saved, our spirit is born again and regenerated by the Holy Spirit, and we inherit access to having His divine nature at the very core of our being:

> *... by which have been given to us exceedingly great and precious promises, that through these you may be partakers of the divine nature...* 2 Peter 1:4

Jesus' perfect righteousness is imputed to us when we are born again. There is an actual spiritual transaction that takes place in the spirit realm. It is not just a mental assent to begin following a moral ideology. This is what sets biblical Christianity apart from *all* other religions.

> *So also it is written, "The first **man**, Adam, **became a living soul**." The last Adam (Jesus Christ) became a **life-giving spirit**.* 1 Corinthians 15:45 *NASB (parenthesis added)*

At salvation, our spirits are made perfect in the eyes of God.

> *For by one sacrifice he has **made perfect** forever those who are being made holy.* Hebrews 10:14 *NIV*

That is our spirit. On the other hand, our soul consists of our mind, will, and emotions—our personality. It is who we are as a person. When we talk about "saving our souls," we include our life force (spirit), as well as who we are as people (soul). When the body dies, the spirit and soul move on until we receive our immortal bodies at the Resurrection. God actually enjoys who we are as people (less the sinful nature and dysfunction), and we will continue to be ourselves throughout eternity, and not some nameless, ambiguous spirits floating around in Heaven. Once there is a final eradication of all vestiges of our sinful human nature, we will be the perfect version of ourselves, reflecting God's glory and perfect redemption and design for eternity.

Because our soul is *not made perfect* upon salvation, it

is still subject to our thinking and opinions, hurts and experiences, and disobedience and weaknesses. Following Jesus is not primarily an intellectual exercise (soul), but a spiritual one, after which we bring our thinking and heart into alignment with our regenerated, born-again spirit.

Sanctification is the process of bringing our souls into submission and alignment with the principles, ways, heart, and spirit of who He is, and our renewed born-again spirit. This is much of the formation of the Christian walk.

So, when you hear the term "soulish," it refers to something that comes from the soul of Man and not the Spirit of God. Often, it is difficult for us to determine from which source it is coming. Especially, when things that are being said and done, which are soulish, sound good and correct, and are not necessarily in contradiction to the Word of God. This happens because our souls are not completely sanctified and are full of mixture. We have opinions and old ways of thinking that are being mixed with the new ways that the Holy Spirit and His Word are teaching us. If we do not become familiar with the Spirit, then we will tend to attribute soulish things to the Spirit, which are not. Let me give you an analogy.

Soulish Dirty Bathwater

Let's say that you have a bathtub full of dirty water with no drain, and that this is symbolic of your soul upon being saved. When you turn on the tap, clean water (things of the Spirit) begins to fill the tub. This is you if, with pure intentions, you commit yourself to the Christian disciplines that enable you to discover more about who God is and what your new life in Christ is all about: prayer, Bible reading/study, water baptism, taking communion, fellowship/discipleship with other believers, giving, learning to serve, etc. As the tub begins to fill with clean water, the dirty water is still there, but the more volume of clean water that flows in dissipates and further dilutes the dirty water. If you were to take a cup and dip it into the tub, you would draw out a mixture of dirty and clean water—some good, some bad. The ratio of clean to dirty water is directly related to the amount of inflow of clean water to which you avail yourself. If you turn the faucet down to a trickle, then you should not expect that much of what you are drawing out is of the Spirit, but more of your own soulish ideas, mixed with a bit of godly truth.

Much, if not a majority of ministry is done in this way by Christians who have not availed themselves to being empowered by the Holy Spirit as the first Church was throughout the Book of Acts, via the baptism of the Holy Spirit. We may give many "good" words, ideas, sermons, and counsel, but it is not necessarily from the Holy Spirit, with the accompanying power. Our results reflect this. If it were, we would be having the Jesus-type successes that *He* promised:

> *Very truly I tell you, whoever believes in me will do the works I have been doing, and they will do even greater things than these, because I am going to the Father.* John 14:12 *NIV*

However, if you hold a cup up as close as possible to the faucet, you will get more pure, clean, untainted water. This is how it is when you are drawing on the Spirit of God, via your spiritual gifts, or "getting into the Spirit", you get closer to the source of the flow. Our goal is to take directly from the Holy Spirit and give it away, untainted by our own soulishness, limited understanding, opinions, abilities, experiences, or current level of sanctification. God has given us spiritual gifts that enable us to get into that place where we draw directly from Him, and praying in tongues is one of those tools.

Religion and religious activities are not the same as the inflow and outflow of the Spirit. We can do all the disciplines that I mentioned, but if the motive and intention is not from a heart that wants to know the Lord in intimacy and includes a surrender to be changed into His likeness, then it will not displace our soulish ways. Anyone can increase in *knowledge about* God, but only true worshippers in Spirit and truth can increase in *personally knowing* God.

The Pharisees, Sadducees, and teachers of the Law memorized God's Word, observed the God-prescribed Feasts and Sabbaths, and centered the entirety of their lives around the Lord. But they were not practicing it out of the desire to be transformed inwardly into His likeness, which requires an active turning from sin and worldly ways. They were open to the information realm—soul and mind—but not the spiritual realm, wherein the power of transformation takes place.

As our proverbial bathtub begins to overflow with the continuous infilling of pure spiritual water, it should continually displace our soulishness. Eventually, what we have to offer is, for the most part, Spirit and truth, and very little of our own humanistic, soulish ideas and reasoning.

Doing things for the Lord from our soul does not require a relationship or sensitivity to a *Person's* leading; it only requires directives or formulas. Wind me up, point me in a direction, and watch me go! This is in stark contrast to Jesus' example, "I only do what I see My Father doing." This is the correct biblical way of following Jesus. We never hear

Christians say, "I want to be led by my soul. I want to be concept and formula-driven!" No, but what we always hear is that we need to be *Spirit-led*. And the Spirit requires supernatural power and faith, which tends to be more work and risk than many of us are willing to take. "Just give us some directives, Lord, and we will be happy to do them for you!" But this is not His best.

A good question to be continually asking yourself is, "Which part of me is leading my life? My body, soul, or spirit?" Is it your carnal desires (body), emotional and intellectual needs, thoughts, desires, and opinions (soul), or your born-again, redeemed spirit? Who's in the driver's seat and calling the shots? Or which is in the pole position driving your life?

I believe that most people who are ignorant of what it means to flow and interact with the reality of the Holy Spirit live their lives and conduct ministry with their soul at the top, with their spirit and body taking orders from how they feel, what they think, and what they need. This is not God's best as it limits us to only that which we naturally know, and how healthy our thought life and emotional state.

Praying in tongues reasserts our spirit into that lead position so that we then process life and operate in ministry in the correct order: spirit, soul, and body. As our perfect born-again spirit is in Christ, we then sow into or strengthen our spirit-man by praying in tongues. That connection with the Holy Spirit, with its assertion, then supersedes our natural limitations and taps into His unlimited ability.

Another example of soul versus spirit is when we are at a church service during the worship (music) time, and we feel lethargic, disconnected, and apathetic. We have all been there. Then, for the final song, the worship team begins playing our favorite worship song. Immediately, our heart begins to soar, we begin to engage, we begin to sing, we raise our hands, and by the end of the song, tears are flowing, and the congregation is whooping and hollering at the conclusion of the song.

Afterwards, we mentioned to a friend how the Spirit was moving during worship. Well... no, not necessarily. The reality is that your soul was moved by the music, specifically your favorite song. If it had not been your favorite song, you probably would not have been moved to that extent or even past half-hearted participation. The soulish affinity for the song that you like causes it to fasten to and lift your emotions… your soul. Your soul was then moved. You see, when our soul dominates us over our spirit, we are moved more by soulish things.

When your spirit is leading your soul, then it wouldn't matter what song was playing, or if any music was playing at all. You will begin to worship in the Spirit and truth, *from* your spirit. The externals do not matter. What you're thinking or feeling does not matter or interfere with your worship. You worship Him for the worth of who He is, regardless of how you're feeling or the surroundings. This can be difficult for most of us to attain regularly, but it is possible. But that's where the power of tongues is of great benefit. Tongues are an immediate express ticket to elevate our spirit above our soul and go directly into the spirit realm. So, if you want to worship in the Spirit *every time*, regardless of the presence or quality of music, then worship and/or sing to Him in tongues.

How to Get into the Spirit

There are examples throughout Scripture of the saints having direct encounters with God and His angels in the natural realm, where there is a physical manifestation of the heavenly on Earth. Just a few examples are:

- Abraham hosting the three "men" outside of Sodom & Gomorrah.
- Moses and the burning bush.
- The Lord descending upon Mount Sinai in clouds of darkness and fire.
- Elisha sees the Chariot of Israel coming down from Heaven and sweeping away Elijah.
- The shepherds in the field see the angelic host rejoicing and announcing the birth of Jesus.

However, most of the heavenly encounters throughout the Bible were "in the spirit", the invisible realm that is the primary abode of God, the angels, and the powers and principalities of evil. These encounters were either sovereignly initiated by the Lord Himself, or they were His reaction to saints seeking His face out of simple devotion or for answers to various life issues.

Some examples of God sovereignly touching the senses of the individual to allow them to see and hear into the spirit realm while awake and still clearly being in their physical bodies were:

- Balaam sees the angel of the Lord blocking the path of his donkey.
- Elisha's servant Gehazi saw the angelic chariots of fire encircling the armies that were surrounding them.
- King David saw the angel striking down Israelites because of the census that He took.

- An angel appears to Cornelius to tell him to fetch Simon Peter.
- Peter's trance vision on the rooftop of the sheet being let down from Heaven.

Most biblical spiritual encounters are through dreams or visions of the spirit realm. Although I am aware of different kinds of visions, for simplicity's sake, I will say that the main difference between dreams and visions is that dreams are given while asleep, and visions are given while you are awake.

However, when we sleep, what does our spirit do? Our spirit never sleeps. It has no need. Our spirit is fully awake and receptive to the spirit realm. This heightened receptivity is possible because our mind, will, and emotions (our soul), with their potential blocks to the Spirit, are, for the most part, taking a siesta. Is it any wonder why the Lord repeatedly uses this time and method to communicate to us and the biblical characters of old, things of such importance?

This is another area of great need in the Body of Christ; the need to equip people to not only recognize from what source their dreams come but also how to interpret them. We miss many warnings, instructions, and revelations from the Father because of our lack of attention to this method of Spirit communication. If you were to ask most congregants how many of them feel that they have had significant dreams, I believe that a majority would raise their hands. Yet these dreams go unattended and unheeded.

Visions are received because a saint has either entered a place of focused attention on the Lord, or they are in a state of continuous flow with the Holy Spirit, and He can show them things of the spirit in a moment, at any moment. In the Old

Testament, the saints did not have the outpouring of the Holy Spirit available to them, and it was only given to them sovereignly by God at specific times for specific purposes. Or, it was given to those that the Lord had designated to fill specific roles in Israel, such as the Prophets.

These powerful visions are recorded throughout the Bible: Ezekiel, Daniel, Isaiah, the Apostle John's revelation on the island of Patmos, and the Apostle Peter's trance vision of the sheet of unclean animals coming down from Heaven are among some of the most well-known. The reality of being in the spirit realm while awake was so intense that the Apostle Paul stated,

> *I know a man in Christ who fourteen years ago—whether in the body I do not know, or whether out of the body I do not know, God knows—such a one was caught up to the third heaven. And I know such a man—whether in the body or out of the body I do not know, God knows—how he was caught up into Paradise and heard inexpressible words, which it is not lawful for a man to utter.* 2 Corinthians 12:2-4

The Apostle John stated,

> *I was in the Spirit on the Lord's day, and heard behind me a great voice, as of a trumpet... Revelation 1:10*

The Apostle Peter was focusing on the Lord when…

> *...he* ***fell into a trance*** *and saw heaven opened and an object like a great sheet...* Acts 10:10-11

I don't believe that any of these men were sitting listening to their favorite worship music to get in the mood or focused on the Lord, and then it happened. But we do know from the

Scriptures that each one of these Church leaders prayed in tongues, or "in the Spirit." There is a reason why it is/was called "praying in the Spirit." It was a way that the saints could shift their focus, at will, from the natural realm to the spirit realm, via the Holy Spirit. And so can you.

In the New Testament, the outpouring of the Holy Spirit, which enables us to enter the spirit realm, is available to "whosoever will" all ages, races, genders, and social status (Acts 2:17). This is the major significance of the baptism of the Holy Spirit. All followers of Jesus are afforded the ability to enter into the spirit realm to see and hear what the Lord is saying and doing. One of the easiest ways to do this is through praying in tongues, bypassing the natural mind and availing your spirit directly to God, who ***is*** spirit.

The Apostle Paul writes to Timothy:

> *Therefore I remind you to* ***<u>stir</u> <u>up</u> the gift of God*** *which is in you* ***through the laying on of my hands***. 2 Timothy 1:6

I used to wonder which one of the nine spiritual gifts Paul was referring to in that verse: prophecy, healing, miracles, word of knowledge, etc. I wondered what specific spiritual gift Timothy operated in that he had to stir up to use.

Then one day, I realized that it wasn't a specific spiritual gift that Paul was talking about. Those gifts are given by the Holy Spirit and not endowed by men. But the one gift that is imparted and received by the laying on of hands is the Holy Spirit Himself, upon the baptism of the Holy Spirit and power. This is confirmed in the next verse,

For God has not given us a spirit of fear, but of power and of love and of a sound mind. 2 Timothy 1:7

The Spirit that is given upon each believer experiencing their own personal Pentecost, "*power from on high,*" is THE Spirit of power, love, and a sound mind, resulting in boldness to be as Christ, as opposed to a spirit of fear that keeps us held back. This is the reason for the baptism of the Spirit—to do what we cannot do in our own strength.

So, how was Timothy to stir up the gift of the Holy Spirit within? Do the one thing that he was given the ability to do upon receiving the baptism in the Holy Spirit: pray in the Spirit! The only spiritual gift that you can initiate on command, at will. That's how you "get into the Spirit." Stir Him up!

The spirit realm is uncomfortable and awkward to our human way of doing things. Our soul likes clearly defined boundaries and established formulas of how to do things and what to expect. "If I do this, then I will have the expected outcome of this, this, and this..." This is summed up by one word... *control.* Our soul likes to be in control and know what to expect. It likes things to make sense—it likes order.

Operation in the spirit realm is not based on cause-and-effect natural principles, but it is based on *relationship,* to either demonic spirits or the Holy Spirit (a Christian versus a witch doctor, for example). As disciples of Jesus Christ, we cannot abandon the spirit realm to the demonic and those humans who work to further their diabolical schemes by settling for just having church meetings and doing ministry by natural, soulish means. I believe and have seen that a moment of ministry by the Spirit can supersede decades of ministry in the natural realm and is the ***only means*** by which demonic strongholds can be broken.

I have ministered to numerous people who have been under spiritual attack, or duress, in their minds and/or emotions. Whether it's anxiety, fear, depression, confusion, agitation, distress, etc., they exclaim, "I pray and I rebuke it, but it just keeps coming at me!" When I ask them if they've prayed in tongues yet, they seem surprised that tongues are even a viable and helpful option.

When the enemy attacks us, it is typically in the soul realm (thoughts and emotions). Whether attacks are demonically inspired or situationally provoked, the attacks manifest primarily in the soul and sometimes even in our bodies. But the one place that it does not affect us is in our born-again spirit. Our spirit is impervious to the attacks of the enemy. There is nothing that the enemy can do to directly affect our spirit-man, so they focus their attacks on the soul, trying to get us to agree with lies and deceptions that stop us from operating and dealing with them in the spirit realm where we reign with Jesus.

If you are being soul-led instead of spirit-led, then the enemy's attacks on you will have a greater effect on you because they are hitting you in the very seat of power from which you live your life.

However, if you pray in the Spirit, you elevate your spirit-man above your soul, connecting with the Holy Spirit. The attacks, or "fiery darts" of the Enemy that normally have a greater impact on the vulnerability of your soul, now must get through your spirit. It is like raising your spirit as a "shield of faith" to extinguish the attacks against your soul as you magnify your spirit above your soul. It's interesting that tongues can act as a shield of faith to your soul, and that it, in and of itself, is completely a *faith gift*. I'll discuss this later in the chapter.

Many people report that after they have shifted from the fruitless mental fighting and rebuking of attacks from the Enemy with no apparent results, they finally obtained relief and peace after praying in tongues. Remember that in Christ, your righteous, born-again spirit is invulnerable and completely dominant over the enemy. Live there and fight from that position!

Are You An Easy Target?
If we are more *Soul-driven* than *Spirit-led* then we are more susceptible to the attacks of the Enemy...
So how can we magnify that which is invulnerable?

Aligning Our Spiritual Satellite Dish

In the 1970's and 1980's, to obtain decent television reception, you either had to have an antenna on the top of your television set or a very large antenna on your rooftop that was connected to your television. These antennas had to be pointed in the direction of the broadcast towers to receive each television station or channel. As technology improved, satellite dishes came into more common use. Satellite reception was clearer because the dishes were pointed toward space, where trees and mountains were no longer objects of interference for broadcast signals.

I want you to imagine that you have a spiritual satellite dish or antenna in your spirit. The truth of the matter is that we all know that there are times when we feel very spiritual and times when we feel anything but spiritual. The truth is that our spiritual standing *is in no way* dependent upon our feelings. However, we live on this earth, and we allow the cares of this world and other unspiritual, natural things (though not necessarily wrong things) to take us out of spiritual awareness and sharpness.

The absolute beauty, and what I believe is the greatest benefit of tongues, is that at any moment a person can willfully choose to engage in the Spirit, turning their "spiritual satellite dish" to the Holy Spirit to pick up what He is essentially broadcasting to us. We join Him in His flow. This is an absolute game-changer for the Christian life!

This ability to "tune in" to the Spirit is a significant advantage that a Spirit-filled tongue-speaking believer has over a non-tongue-speaking believer. What I am not saying is that someone who speaks in tongues is a stronger or better believer than a believer who doesn't speak in tongues. I am saying that Christians who have availed themselves of receiving this ability to align, connect, and elevate their spirit-man supernaturally to the Holy Spirit, at will, regardless of emotions or knowledge and circumstance, have an advantage over someone who has to rely solely on their past experience, scriptural knowledge, and what they can see or discern with their natural eyes and ears—their soul.

Here are some common Christian-life examples that may help to put this into a practical perspective:

Prayer Meetings - I teach equipping seminars on how to have effective corporate and intercessory prayer. If you were to ask every church/Christian in the world what the top three most important things to do as a follower of Jesus Christ, prayer would be in the top three, if not the number one thing. Yet, for all this apparent agreement, the church prayer meeting is most often the least attended and least consistent church event that we hold. It is also true that most churches do not even hold a weekly prayer meeting. Why is this? Well, there are many reasons, but I believe the core reason is the absence of Spirit-led liveliness in prayer that produces results.

Many prayer meetings are soulish because they are not led or made up of people who know how to get into the Spirit. Usually, it is relegated to running down the church prayer list of all the known local needs and just reading them back to God. What often happens is that the first part of the meeting, in addition to the prayer list, consists of any need that may come into the participants' minds. Often, jumping around sporadically from missionaries in Africa to praying for the President, to Aunt Suzie's diabetes, to asking for an increase in church attendance. Jumping around from topic to topic can be dizzying, as each of the prayer givers is verbalizing anything and everything that comes to mind (soul) from moment to moment. The result is typically a general light crop-dusting of mentionables that we feel good about because we seem to have covered all the Church's and world's needs. Yet, there has been no "praying through" on any given topic. It is a valuing of shallow quantity over depth of quality because there is no awareness that there is a deeper, more effective level of prayer, which can move proverbial mountains.

My wife tells of her bedtime prayers when she was a little girl. Before she would go to sleep, she felt that if she did not name every single person and need that she knew of, then something bad was going to happen to them. Of course, this is an immature (and exhausting) understanding of how prayer works. But this is also the way that many prayer meetings are conducted; not so much from the fear aspect, but having to have a cursory mentioning of everything, which shows an equal lack of spiritual maturity.

But at least that type of prayer meeting has some form of activity. What I have seen very regularly is that after the opening prayer, everyone sits quietly trying to hear God. Deferring to His leading is the correct course of action, but if there's nobody who knows how to press into the Spirit for that direction, we'll sit. I have sat in meetings for 40 minutes while everyone tried to hear something from God. Then, eventually, a couple of half-hearted prayers were offered up because, well, we have to pray something to account for the last hour. You might be thinking, "Well, doesn't God say, 'to be still and know that I am God?'" Well, that's taking that verse out of context. All I know is that if I told my wife that I wanted to spend an hour with her talking to her in-depth about what was going on in our lives, and I was silent the whole time with my head nodding off repeatedly, fighting sleepiness, she would not be happy with me! She wants my engaged dialogue, not my spousal obligation. Besides, our Father is not playing a game with us to see how long we can "wait upon the Lord" before we get bored and quit. He is ready to, and wants to speak, at a moment's notice. But do we know how to hear and engage with Him?

When I attend a Spirit-filled and led prayer meeting, where the participants are praying in tongues personally, we all begin to tune in individually to the Holy Spirit. There then becomes a greater awareness of whether the manifest presence of God enters the room and recognition when someone is bringing forth a word or prayer from the Holy Spirit. I like to say that we can tell when someone "has the ball"—when the anointing is upon, or the Spirit is flowing through somebody. When you think about it, it is a bit like rugby; whoever has "the ball" runs with it. When they're done, someone else picks it up and runs with it until they are done. Every participant has their receptors turned toward the Holy Spirit by praying in tongues while simultaneously listening with their minds to the person praying. Tongues allow you to do both easily. Often, the Spirit will give you something to pray or prophesy that piggybacks off of what is currently being prayed by someone else. We let the Spirit let us know when we are finished praying for a particular topic. When the general sense in the spirit realm is that there is nothing more that He has for us, then we are done with that topic.

When all the people involved are in tune in this way, you will find that as a group, you will pray through certain issues much more thoroughly and effectively. Often, we'll receive new revelation from God as to how to specifically pray to bring a resolution or receive a promise, instruction, or encouragement from the Lord as to the outcome. Afterward, the group's sense that something significant was accomplished in the spirit realm is very gratifying. "Now that was a prayer meeting!" It invokes excitement and passion to attend the next prayer meeting because you know that something good always happens.

<u>Worship Services & Atmospheres</u> - I love anointed worship music. Do you ever wonder why worship services *always* start with musical worship? "Because we're supposed to 'enter into His gates with thanksgiving, and into His courts with praise'. And 'He inhabits the praises of His people.'" Well, can't you do that without music? You sure can. Tell me which of the Twelve Disciples carried a lute or lyre on his back? I mean, today, if we were going to go out as a group for God or meet in a home, *somebody* must bring a guitar or a smartphone with music on it. How else are we going to have worship?!

The main reason why we start with music is because of what I stated earlier... because the Church, in general, is not taught about how to get into the spirit supernaturally. Music is an important tool that connects with our souls (mind/will/emotions), which in turn can lead to helping us to then connect spiritually with God. How often have you needed at least 5-10 minutes of worship songs to settle down your mind or pull you out of the "rat race" mentality to be able to focus on the Lord? This is done to get the people in a mindset that can better receive the preaching of the Word of God. This certainly helps us to get centered, but it does not necessarily get us into the Spirit. Music can be very spiritual, but it first, primarily, moves the soul. It can cause us to cry at the thought of our love for the Lord, but a love song can also make the unbeliever cry at the thought of their girlfriend or boyfriend. That is not entering the spirit realm. The goal should be to get into His manifest Presence by the Spirit, whether accompanied by music or not. But when you are in His manifest Presence, with anointed music, singing, and/or dance, it can be rapturous!

But let me show you how vulnerable we are to being hindered from entering into His Presence by solely relying on the musical aspect of a time of worship, without us individually knowing how to get into the spirit.

Here is a list of the most common obstacles that all of us have experienced at one time or another when we have an immature understanding of the difference between the soul and the spirit, and thus an overreliance on needing to be moved in our soul by music before being able to get into His manifest Presence by the Spirit:

- The worship team or leader is not very musically gifted or off-key.
- The song selection, or music set, is songs you don't know.
- The words to the songs are not on the screen, so you have trouble following along and entering in.
- The leader is more focused on eliciting a response from the crowd than on themselves worshipping.
- The leader spends more time talking between songs than worshipping.
- Someone on the worship team is wearing something inappropriate.
- The worship feels like a performance and not authentic.

If you've spent any length of time in the Body of Christ, you've been affected by these things. But hear me when I say that there is a higher way that doesn't rely so much on the abilities of men!

Many people can attend a service and not even realize that there was no manifest Presence of God during the entire meeting. And how would they know it if they have not been taught to be sensitive or responsive to it, let alone how to get there themselves? We have some work to do. And what most people don't realize is that praying in the Spirit is a major part of this! No wonder there is so much offense and prejudice around the entire topic of speaking in tongues, and it is such a target of the Enemy.

Instead of depending on the worship team or leader to lead me into the Presence of God by first "massaging" my soul for 5-10 minutes, so that I feel like I'm in His Presence, I know how to get there myself, without the music, aside from emotions, feelings, or atmosphere. This is <u>mature</u>, <u>spiritual</u> Christianity!

Jesus carried the atmosphere of heaven (Holy Spirit) within Himself. He was constantly going into situations that were difficult and even hostile to everything that He represented. Thus, He was not *dependent* on the outer atmosphere to accomplish the Father's will in the moment. His inner atmosphere (the Presence) had to be stronger than every outer atmosphere that He stepped into.

However, the outer atmosphere could either lend to working with Him or against Him in accomplishing the desired results He wanted to manifest.

We see this when He visited His hometown of Nazareth (Mt. 13:38, Mk. 6:5). The atmosphere of unbelief hindered Him from doing "*many mighty works there*", because they were offended at this "local boy" purporting to be someone special. But even though the atmosphere hindered Him from doing more, He was able to lay hands on a few sick people and heal them, because of what *He* carried.

Again, when He went to raise Jairus's daughter from death, the mourners laughed and ridiculed Him severely for saying that she was just sleeping. He then took control of the surroundings and put everyone out of the house except for the girl's parents and His top three leaders: Peter, James, and John. He removed the unbelief that would more hinder than help what He knew the Father wanted to do.

Whenever I enter a worship service, I begin to pray in tongues quietly to align my spirit with the Holy Spirit to see what He is saying and doing. I do not speak out loud enough for others to hear me because it is not for them, it is for me. I will go back and forth between praying in the Spirit and singing worship songs. I find that worshipping in tongues is much more effective and expedient because it bypasses my mind and emotions completely, so I do not have to fight through those things to give to the Lord what He deserves or to receive from Him directly or through His ministers on the platform. This also heightens my ability to recognize whether His manifest Presence comes into the place or if there is something that is off or blocking this from happening.

Often, you will be used to begin praying against specific things that you sense are hindering His Presence from coming. With this, you have transitioned from being a Christian *consumer*, who just goes to church to get something, to being a Christian *producer*, who is there to give something. I know that leaders, preachers, and worship leaders are truly grateful for those people in the congregation who are equipped, aware, and available to intercede for the needed atmosphere. As disciples of Jesus Christ, we are all called to be aware of the spirit realm at this level. And why wouldn't you want to be?

Small Groups & Gatherings – My wife and I regularly attend many gatherings of saints in smaller and more intimate venues than a typical church service. When we come together in praise and worship, music can be a large part of it, but it is also intermixed with prayer, declarations, prophetic utterances, and praying in tongues corporately. Because we have established a community of believers who are mature and familiar with the moving of the Spirit, there are many times that we may only play one or two songs before we get into the Spirit, His Presence, by praying and singing in the Spirit (tongues) together. Very quickly, the atmosphere of the room shifts, and His Presence falls on all of us. We then minister to Him and each other out of His manifest Presence.

When you have a group of people who do not require soulish stimuli to be convinced to emotionally feel God's Presence, but they know how to step into their inheritance by the Spirit, by faith, you just aren't emotionally moved by the process, but you tangibly feel the actual manifestation of His Presence—His weightiness, His glory. Then, from that place, remarkable and supernatural things can happen.

Circumcision of the Soul Through Praying in Tongues

The concept of circumcision, both literal and spiritual, is significant throughout the Bible. Circumcision was the cutting away of the male foreskin as a physical sign of the covenantal agreement between God and man/people.

In the New Testament, the idea of circumcision is applied to our spiritual walk with the Lord and represents the new covenantal agreement between all men and God, when entered into through faith in Jesus Christ.

I believe that multiple revelations stem from the concept of circumcision, and one specifically as it relates to praying in tongues:

- Abrahamic/Mosaic Circumcision - a cutting away of the foreskin with a knife, to mark the physical flesh as a sign of a covenantal relationship with God.

- New Testament Circumcision - a spiritual inward circumcision of the heart that the Gospel produces by the cutting away of the fleshly, sinful nature. The result of this regeneration produces righteous living through a believer's covenant with God through Christ.
- Circumcision of the Mind - a cutting away of our former worldly thinking by the application of the Word of God (the sword of the spirit), making it obedient to Christ through the renewing of our mind into the mind of Christ.
- Circumcision of the Soul - a cutting away of operating by the wisdom, precepts, and methods of man that is accomplished by praying in the Holy Spirit (tongues), exalting our spirit above our souls. (Matthew 17:20-21)

Our God-Given Spiritual Weight Set

In a gym, as you lift various weights, you tear down soft, flabby muscle and cause it to rebuild itself bigger, harder, and stronger than what was there previously. Analogously, each time you "lift weights" or "work out" spiritually, then you are tearing down naturalistic human thinking and reasoning, fleshly/worldly desires, and unhealthy emotional states; and you are replacing them with the strong, healthy, tested, dependable, timeless, and unfailing precepts of God and His Kingdom.

In the church, God has provided each of us with various natural gifts with which to serve Him: teaching, preaching, giving, discernment, helps, hospitality, wisdom, leadership, administration/organization, mercy/compassion, etc. These are referred to as *motivational gifts* and can cover a broad spectrum. Motivational gifts are usually indicative of the way God has wired a person and what areas of service that person is energized by or motivated to do, with an accompanying aptitude.

In addition, nine supernatural spiritual gifts are mentioned: prophecy, speaking in tongues, interpretation of tongues, faith, healing, miracles, word of wisdom, word of knowledge, and discerning of spirits.

Of the nine spiritual gifts, every single gift's primary function is for the benefit and strengthening of *others,* except one. There is one spiritual gift whose primary function is for the benefit and strengthening of *oneself.*

> *He who speaks in a tongue edifies (builds up, strengthens) himself... (v. 4)* (parenthesis added)

Thus, praying in tongues, in essence, can be considered your *spiritual weight set*! It is paramount to the theme of this entire book that you understand the significance of what this means…

If God has given me a spirit or heavenly language to pray and praise, spirit-to-Spirit whenever I want to, and in so doing I spiritually strengthen and build up myself each time by praying out spiritual mysteries to God (which bypasses my natural lack of understanding), then why would I not want to be doing it continually and helping other Christians to do the same?

The more you lift, the stronger you become. Or more specifically, the more spiritually flexible and attuned you become. Why do you think the Apostle Paul said:

"I wish that you all spoke with tongues..." (v.5)

> *"I thank my God I speak with tongues more than you all..."* (v.18)

It would be no different from a strong, fit person saying to a bunch of us overweight, out-of-shape folks, "I wish that you all would make the time to get into the gym at least sometime during the week. I thank God that I make it a priority to work out 4-5 times a week." And the difference spiritually is no less obvious than the difference in the physical appearances of our respective bodies.

If, in most churches, for a myriad of reasons, powerlessness in the Spirit is the accepted norm, how would anyone know that we are spiritually scrawny when our entire church community judges itself by itself, instead of by the biblical standard? It is easy to unobtrusively blend into the midst of a group of people who are just like us.

Which one of us who is out-of-shape wants to go to the pool or beach, pull up a lounge chair, and plop our squeezable softness next to the most chiseled guy or the most toned, cross-fit, young lady around? No thanks. I'm on vacation, not auditioning for the "before" picture on a total makeover reality show.

Yet, we are called to be thoroughly like Jesus. Not just in spiritual fruit and character, but in spiritual power and might. If spiritual power were muscles, Jesus would be an imposing figure, garnering the admiration of all in our circumference. And if we are honest about it, we would not be able to run with Him and his first disciples in their work if we were not willing to step it up and pack on some muscle for ourselves. Jesus actually *required it* from them even before the Day of Pentecost while they were ministering with Him, and when He sent them out by twelve, and then by seventy.

People who have toned, muscular, and in-shape bodies have it because they spend time lifting weights. Distance runners may be in shape, but they do not necessarily have muscle. Just as muscular people may not necessarily have endurance. Strength training builds muscle, and cardio training builds endurance. Likewise, spiritual strength builds power, whereas spiritual character builds endurance. This helps us understand why there are people who pray in tongues and move in spiritual gifts, but who are still working through some character issues or lack of spiritual maturity.

God wants to baptize you with the Holy Spirit (B.O.T.H.S.) immediately upon conversion (it does not happen automatically) and give you the ability to speak in tongues for your spiritual strengthening, even as a newborn babe in Christ. You will then develop spiritual character and endurance as you walk with Him through the years, adhering to the tenets of His Word and His ways.

When I'm ministering to people: the sick, the broken, the oppressed, the needy, etc., I would rather have a baby Christian who has received the infilling of the Holy Spirit and power accompanying me, than a seasoned believer who has not yet entered into or received this aspect of the Kingdom of God. The reason for this is that the new believer has not learned limitations on what God can do through them and their spiritual gifts. Even though they are newly born-again, they have the raw ability and power to hear from and operate by the Spirit. Though, as with most gifts and talents, they may need a little coaching in the application.

Conversely, the seasoned believer who has not received the BOTHS probably has a ton more bible knowledge, wisdom, and maturity, but has not yet received the knowledge of what their spiritual gifts are (not motivational gifts, but supernatural spiritual gifts), nor have they received the empowerment by which to operate in them. Sadly, I used to minister in this way. When ministering, I would talk people to death with bible verses because I had no power or anointing to help them like Jesus and His first disciples did. It is a very big deal because *"the yoke shall be destroyed because of the anointing."* Isaiah 10:27 *KJV*. We must receive the Lord's anointing to achieve the Lord's results!

If we claim that we truly love people, then each of us must deal with this deficiency in our lives of re-presenting Jesus Christ. It is completely illogical that any Christian would not want, or be resistant to, receiving and operating in the only spiritual gift whose main purpose is to strengthen oneself in their inner spirit man.

Drinking Your Faith Shakes

Anyone who seriously lifts weights knows that protein is *the* basic nutrient in building our muscles. When you lift weights, you tear down the muscle you're targeting. After exertion, your muscle begins to rebuild itself using proteins from your body to do so. For this reason, protein powder shakes and drinks are big business within the fitness industry. Without a steady supply of protein, workouts will just make you worn out.

Similarly, faith is to our spiritual strength what protein is to muscle. Faith is *the* key and *the* catalyst to how everything works in the Kingdom of God. Every spiritual work and gift is done by faith. Love is the motivation—the ***why***. Faith is the operation—the ***how***.

For proof that faith is the key component needed to see supernatural Kingdom results, one only has to look at Jesus throughout the Gospels. Wherever He went, He was constantly looking for faith to connect with it. He was always urging those who needed to receive a miracle to "only believe," or to "have faith in God." He always marveled at and praised those who showed great faith. Conversely, He admonished His Disciples often when they did not have the faith that was required to follow in His footsteps and get His results.

> *"But, without faith it is impossible to please Him."* Hebrews 11:6.

So, if we want to be strong in spirit, we need to increase our faith. Scripture tells us two ways that we can grow in faith:

> *So then faith comes by* **hearing**, *and hearing by the word of God.* Romans 10:17

Firstly, you can grow your faith by having an open heart that will hear what the Word of God says to you, and then *apply it*. Changing your thinking to and setting your subsequent course by it will cause you to grow in faith.

Secondly, there is a supernatural way to grow in faith:

> *But you, beloved, building yourselves up on your most holy faith,* ***praying in the Holy Spirit***... Jude 20

Once again, we see yet another biblical author reminding us that praying in the Spirit builds us up in our spirit-man—our faith.

Every biblical example of someone who was filled with the Holy Spirit immediately included praising God in other tongues. There is a reason for this. Tongues, as a prayer/praise language, is the first, most basic, and simplest of the supernatural spiritual gifts. It is the easiest to receive and operate in because, upon the infilling of the Holy Spirit, it wells up from within you, from your spirit. It is your spirit crying out to and praising God in a spirit language, usually in response to the power of His presence upon the BOTHS. It is the gateway to all of the other gifts because getting you connected with the Lord Himself on a deeper spiritual level is of foundational importance for everything else.

Staying Loose & Flowing with the Holy Spirit

I was a three-sport athlete in high school and then went on to play football in college. And there was one thing that was non-negotiable in every sport—stretching and warm-ups. All sports do this to better avoid the injury of pulling a muscle. But also, staying loose enables you to perform to the best of your athletic ability. It helps you access your full range of motion, top speed, and optimal strength of muscles. Praying in tongues is synonymous with stretching and staying "loose" in the spirit.

Shortly after I had received the BOTHS, I took part in a large outdoor crusade in San Diego where an evangelist from Argentina came and held a five-night crusade. I was working in the "Deliverance Tent," the place where people with demons go to have them cast out. It was likened to a freak show under an actual red and white circus tent. I saw some crazy things, and I was very hungry to learn and experience more of the realities of the Kingdom of God into which I had just recently stepped. I had had a powerful infilling of the Spirit and spoke in tongues, but I had not yet learned how to really flow with Him. I was working through many offenses to my religious sensibilities as I was having all of these new experiences with God and being exposed to Spirit-filled Christian ministry.

We ministered to the demonized in groups of three. I was new to the whole "Spirit-filled" thing, so I was still ministering in my old way of reciting scripture verses to solve every person's need. Got a problem? Well, I got a verse for that! By God and by His Word, I am going to fix you!!!

After we finished ministering to a person, the only female in our group, who was the most effective and anointed out of the three of us, addressed me. "You're pretty intense. You must understand that the Holy Spirit is light, and not so intense. There is an ease and flow about Him. You've gotta lighten up!" Considering her apparent successes and my slogging my way through the ministry mud, I knew she had thrown me a valuable nugget. Before the week was through, I had a brief encounter with God, which was a key breakthrough moment for me in learning how to receive from and flow with the Holy Spirit.

Since then, I have learned that when ministering to people, we must lead with our spirit, not our heads (knowledge)… and not even our hearts (emotions). Truly, the Spirit of God moves as a flow. And to get into that flow with Him is of utmost importance if we want to get Jesus-level results. Remember, the Holy Spirit is "a mighty rushing wind." Feathers are taken with the wind; cement blocks are not.

Jesus said that out of our spirits *rivers* of living water will *flow*. In the book of Revelations, it is not the Lake of Life, nor the Pond or Pool of Peace… it is the *River of Life*. And it flows from under the very Throne of God, to us, and out of our spirit to others. If you cannot get into this flow, you will not give people everything that they need, nor everything that their Heavenly Father desires to give them.

Sowing to the Spirit regularly by praying in tongues keeps you aware and responsive to His flow. It elevates your spirit above your soul (mind, will, emotions, personality).

I am not aware of anyone that I know personally, or for that matter have even heard of, who moves in consistent, supernatural, spiritual power and does not pray in tongues. And I do not mean a person who is a powerful preacher or teacher! That is not a *spiritual* gift. That is a gift from God, but it is not one of the nine spiritual gifts. There are powerful public speakers and teachers who are unsaved. Every person who is used powerfully and consistently in supernatural healing, miracles, prophecy, faith, word of knowledge, etc.... speaks in tongues. I have yet to know of anyone who moves in these things at any significant level who does not pray in tongues. One is linked to the other because your ability to flow in other spiritual gifts is affected by praying in tongues.

Your faith increases when you pray in tongues because tongues are the ultimate faith gift. It only operates by faith, and faith alone. So, when you choose to operate in this primary spiritual gift, which at its core requires complete faith to operate in, your faith will increase as you work your "faith muscle."

God's Ingenious Bypass

On page 115, *Becoming Foolish to Become Wise*, I showed that our biggest obstacle to receiving and moving in the things of the Spirit is our minds—our human reasoning and understanding. Of this, Scripture minces no words. There we discussed that, according to Paul, when we pray in tongues, "our mind is unfruitful." Fantastic! If my mind hinders me from flowing with the Holy Spirit, then I want it out of the way as much as possible. So, how do I bypass it?

> *But the natural man does not receive the things of the Spirit of God, for they are foolishness to him; nor can he know them, because they are spiritually discerned.*
> 1 Corinthians 2:14

> *Because the carnal mind is enmity* (an enemy) *against God...* Romans 8:7 (parenthesis added)

If you go to YouTube, you can find an ABC News report on a medical study that was done by the University of Pennsylvania on speaking in tongues. What they discovered corroborated exactly what the Bible teaches regarding speaking in tongues. When asked to pray in English, the subject's frontal lobe, the part of the brain from which language originates, was very active, as expected. However, when the subject prayed in the Spirit, there was almost no frontal lobe activity whatsoever. Once again, scientific discovery strengthens biblical truth.

Another noteworthy part of the segment was the mention of other studies that were performed on both Buddhist Monks while meditating and Franciscan Nuns while praying. The studies showed that there was a significant increase in brain activity, particularly in the frontal lobes, of both, which indicated an "intense focus," which was in "stark contrast" to what they found in those who prayed in tongues. This scientific proof further shows the validity of what the Bible already teaches us on the difference between the soul and spirit.

I rejoice in this! We are instructed in Scripture to **both** *meditate* on His Word (to renew our mind) and to *pray in the Spirit* (to strengthen our spirit-man). In doing this, we will ready ourselves to better walk in Spirit *and* truth. Feed your spirit with the Spirit, equally as much as you feed your mind with the truth. To not do this will cause us to be unnecessarily weak in an area where God has given us the means by which to be strong.

Faith, Foolishness & the Upside-Down Kingdom

Have you ever wondered why in the world God would choose something like giving us the ability to speak in an unknown spiritual language that either: 1) we do not understand, or 2) only others occasionally would understand as a miraculous sovereign sign to them, or 3) only another person with the specific gift of interpretation in operation could understand? I mean, humanly speaking … what's the point? Well, to me, that sounds exactly like something God would do. It takes it into the *faith realm*. In Scripture, He gives detailed reasons as to why it is useful in so many ways, why it is a valuable heavenly treasure, and why He chose it. But you must search for the buried treasure of understanding and pursue it with faith. Unfortunately, many believers stop at, "What's the point?"

> *Again, the kingdom of heaven is like treasure hidden in a field, which a man found and hid; and for joy over it he goes and sells all that he has and buys that field. Matthew 13:44*

> *It is the glory of God to conceal a matter, but the glory of kings is to search out a matter. Proverbs 25:2*

So, it is ingenious of the Lord, and particularly in His character, to pick something as seemingly foolish as speaking in tongues as a way to strengthen ourselves in the Spirit. The Bible is full of seemingly unreasonable contradictions:

- A virgin giving birth.
- The King of Kings was born in a stable.
- The Holy One is the friend of sinners.
- Saying that those who can see are blind.
- Forgetting what you think you know and becoming like a child, knowing nothing.
- Giving away as a way of receiving more.
- Losing something to find something.
- Going low to be elevated.
- Giving blessings when cursed.
- Serving to reign.
- Becoming foolish to become wise.
- Dying to live.

So, when I operate in this spiritual gift:

- if I must humble myself and do something that may make me look and sound foolish.
- if I am initiating and choosing to exercise it of my own free will, at any time.
- if my mind is unfruitful, and I do not know, nor am I consciously directing, what I am saying.
- if the source of the words is from the depths of my spirit.
- if the actual words that are made are a miraculous work of the Holy Spirit.

- if I am praying out the mysteries of God.
- if I am building up my spirit man and my most holy faith.
- if there is NO EVIDENCE in the natural that any of the above is true except that the WORD OF GOD SAYS SO…

…then I think that qualifies as the ultimate "faith gift."

This is the child-like faith that Jesus says that we need to enter the Kingdom of God, and subsequently, into the deeper things of that Kingdom as well. So, do you see how when you do exercise this gift, believing what the Word teaches about it, you will grow in faith?

> *"Abraham believed God and it was accounted to him as righteousness."* (Romans 4:3).

It gave God glory when Abraham believed that what God had promised would come to pass just because God said so. And God gloried in Abraham's faith. Why would He do any less with the promised gift to the Church Age?

> *"With men of other tongues and other lips I will speak to this people; and yet, for all that, they will not hear Me..."* 1 Corinthians 14:21

This gift is a supernatural sign to the unbeliever that we have received something from the Heavenly Kingdom. That our belief is not just another moral ideology, but it is a "new and living way," full of the Spirit and life, "and yet for all that, they will not hear Me."

I have read so much angry commentary on internet discussion forums from Christians who do not speak in tongues. As such, they do not understand its use, benefits, or the faith aspect of it. One gentleman commented, "You people who pray in tongues need to stop being so lazy and actually talk to your Heavenly Father." A comment like this obviously comes from someone who does not see any *apparent* benefits from tongues (which would be ignorance of Scripture), nor understands the faith aspect of its operation, which is often disdained for its seemingly foolish manifestations. Such are *many aspects* of the Kingdom of God and not only speaking in tongues.

Analogously, it is like a Christian who has yet to enter into faith regarding tithing/giving. Until they understand what the Bible says about giving to God, and until they have *taken steps* to increase their faith in that area through its application, it will seem utterly foolish to them.

For example:

"What? I have $1000 in past due bills, and I have $800 in the bank, and I'm supposed to give God $80 !?! How's that gonna work ?!?"

Well… faith… *because He said so.*

> *For the wisdom of this world is foolishness with God..."* 1 Corinthians 3:9

> *But God has chosen the* ***foolish things*** *of the world to put to shame the wise...* 1 Corinthians 1:27

How to Pray Without Ceasing

Twice in his letters, Paul gives instructions to the saints:

> *Rejoice always, pray without ceasing, in everything give thanks; for this is the will of God in Christ Jesus for you. 1* Thessalonians 5:16-18

> *With all prayer and petition* ***pray at all times in the Spirit,*** *and with this in view, be on the alert with all perseverance and petition for all the saints...* Ephesians 6:18 *NASB*

Because of God's ingenious bypass with the gift of tongues, this is possible more than you might think. Let's be honest, when we sit down to pray (aside from a time of major life crisis), the typical person can pray for about 5-15 minutes before they have run out of things for which to pray. That's because we are *thinking* about what we need to pray for… from our minds. Since praying in tongues does not come from our minds but from our spirit, articulated by the power of the Holy Spirit, then we can pray for hours on end. Because your mind is taken out of the equation, you can pray and think of or do other things.

The next time you're working around the house, driving in your car, or in the shower, try praying in tongues. It is a great way to make spiritual use of the mundane things we must do in everyday life. As was mentioned earlier in this book, sometimes you will pray in tongues in your sleep, as your spirit never needs sleep. And, because it is redeemed and one with the Father through Christ, it longs for Him.

Here is a mindblower (pun intended). There are times when we need to pray in a given situation, but we cannot pray out loud and often do not even know what to pray. *You can pray in tongues silently in your head.* "Hey, wait a minute! I thought you'd been saying this whole time that tongues bypass your mind!" Yes, the mind is unfruitful, and we do not *understand* what is being said, but we do *hear it.* This is about the source from which tongues come. It comes from your spirit, yet is still perceived by your mind, just as your ears perceive and hear it as it comes out of your mouth.

When I think thoughts in my mind, those thoughts are in English and they originate from my mind, so therefore, I am directing those thoughts. When I pray in tongues silently, I can hear the words come into my mind from my spirit, yet I cannot tell you what the next word will be. Additionally, I could write down each word on paper after it was said in my spirit, although it would be written down phonetically (how the word sounds) because it is not a known language, it is a spirit language.

Typically, when I pray in tongues silently, my tongue is moving in my mouth while I am doing it, but not always. It is like my tongue is still doing the motions, but with no sound, but my mind can hear every word as clearly as if I were saying it out loud. Can you see how awesome and useful this is when you find yourself in a situation where you need to pray, but you cannot do it out loud? Most people offer up a silent prayer of, "Lord, Help!" But for someone open to operating in their prayer language as a way of life, you can be praying continually in the Spirit as the drama unfolds in front of you.

For instance, imagine yourself being called into your boss's office, and standing next to him/her is a coworker or your supervisor who has always had it out for you for whatever reason. You are then blindsided by an accusation that this person has concocted by twisting certain truths into half-truths, which make you look very bad. You are completely taken unaware, and there is some truth to what is being said, but it is being twisted to wrong conclusions. Your blood pressure rises, and you fight the urge to either verbally tear into this person (which would not look good to the boss) or try to explain that they are twisting the truth around to make you look bad (which could also not look good to the boss). What do you do?

Well, I don't know. It's hypothetical. But I know that you cannot dismiss yourself to go into the bathroom for the next 5-10 minutes to pray and get the mind of the Lord regarding it. But, if you have sown into living a lifestyle of the Spirit by using this tool, you know that you can be in communication with Him, silently, and begin aligning your spirit and soul with His, as the problem occurs. Simply awesome, and wonderfully useful.

To further shed light on this ability, I will tell you this next story, but you must remember what I have mentioned earlier: receiving the baptism of the Holy Spirit (BOTHS) is not a "fix-all". Empowerment by the Holy Spirit is immediate. Character, or sanctification, is a process of walking with the Holy Spirit in obedience.

There is a precious woman whom my wife and I led into the BOTHS when she was in her early twenties and have mentored her off and on through various seasons when she would seek us out. Regardless of the powerful and profound call on her life, this young lady, since childhood, had many struggles with her identity, self-image, self-worth, and how to healthily relate to men in her life. These struggles often manifested in poor choices and self-injurious behaviors like cutting, drunkenness, drug use, promiscuity, and rebellion in general.

Her choices had landed her in jail multiple times. She would be the first to tell you that through it all, the Lord never left her. She would tell of the frequent feeling of being pursued by Him, even amid her sin. She knew that *she* was the one rejecting Him because of not wanting to submit to what He wanted for her, not that she was the one being rejected.

When we first introduced her to what it was like to walk and connect with the Holy Spirit, she fully embraced speaking in tongues and would do it regularly, knowing and sensing the powerful connection. She recounts the multiple times that she was about to decide whether or not to enter into sinful behaviors or to even act on suicidal thoughts. She said that in her head, she would begin hearing herself praying in tongues and that it was like hearing your favorite song playing in your head that you couldn't stop. It didn't matter whether she wanted to obey or not. She said, "Earlier in my walk, tongues had become so second nature to me that I couldn't get away from it, even if I did not want to be obedient."

Now, theologically speaking, you see that her spirit within her was crying out to God, "deep cries out unto deep." She was even hearing in her mind, her spirit praying in tongues. This exhibits the very wrestling match that Paul describes in Romans 7:14-25:

> *We know that the law is spiritual; but I am unspiritual, sold as a slave to sin. 15 I do not understand what I do. For what I want to do I do not do, but what I hate I do. 16 And if I do what I do not want to do, I agree that the law is good. 17 As it is, it is no longer I myself who do it, but it is sin living in me. 18 For I know that good itself does not dwell in me, that is, in my sinful nature. For I have the desire to do what is good, but I cannot carry it out. 19 For I do not do the good I want to do, but the evil I do not want to do—this I keep on doing. 20 Now if I do*

what I do not want to do, it is no longer I who do it, but it is sin living in me that does it.

[21] *So I find this law at work: Although I want to do good, evil is right there with me.* [22] *For in my inner being I delight in God's law;* [23] *but I see another law at work in me, waging war against the law of my mind and making me a prisoner of the law of sin at work within me.* [24] *What a wretched man I am! Who will rescue me from this body that is subject to death?* [25] *Thanks be to God, who delivers me through Jesus Christ our Lord!* NIV

She told me that, "Even in my darkest times, I knew how to connect with God when I had nothing else. Tongues saved my life."

I have a similar story from a brother who also had powerful encounters with the Lord early in his twenties, after having struggled with his identity and drug use previously. Though soft-hearted towards the Lord, he made a very big mistake one day, which landed him in state prison for five years.

He told me stories of being in prison. There were some serious challenges to his spiritual and especially physical life: gangs, hits, murders, drugs, Satan worshipers, and black magic practitioners who used demon summoning, curses, pacts, and oaths openly in prison.

He told me how the occultists would give him small pamphlets on the black arts each time that they would give him drugs, like the antithesis of a Christian giving out a Gospel tract to win souls. He said that in prison, it is hard to be a Christian because you will be seriously challenged and tested constantly, and for some time, he ignored God.

This young man told me of a time when he and his cellmate were doing speed. As he was lying on his bunk, he felt an evil presence enter the cell. Then, he said that he began to feel a crushing force from both the bottom of his bunk and on top of his chest. He says that he knew that this entity was trying to kill him. Panicking, the only thing that came to his mind was to begin praying in tongues. As he did, the demon released him and left the cell. Immediately afterward, the occultist inmates who were just down the hall yelled and asked him specifically if he had felt anything come into his cell. He told them no (which perplexed them) because he did not want to encourage any more of what they were doing.

From that time on, he said that he was not afraid of the demonic powers that were being invoked in the prison, as he knew, and was reminded of how the superior power of Jesus, through the working of the Holy Spirit, triumphs over these things. This reality check of the eternal spiritual struggle was enough to propel him to reconnect with God through praying in tongues and reading his Bible. God has since used him to preach in prison while he was there. He is now living and serving on a men's recovery ranch here in Southern California. He credits his early years of learning how to connect with the Holy Spirit via speaking in tongues (regardless of what is going on in his spiritual walk at any given time) with saving his physical and spiritual life while in prison.

The value of these things and the mysteries that they unlock in the spirit realm cannot be understated. This is why it grieves me so much when I hear uninformed, non-tongues-speaking Christians bad-mouthing speaking in tongues and tainting others' perception of it. It is quite simply discrediting and disregarding something powerful and useful that's given to us by God Himself, for our own benefit. Precious saint, where is the fear of the Lord in our thinking, opinions, words, and teaching about these things?

Chapter Nine

"How Can I Pray the Will of God When I Don't Know What It Is?"

How to Get Your Prayers Answered

> *This is the confidence we have in approaching God: that if we ask anything according to his will, he hears us. And if we know that he hears us—whatever we ask—we know that we have what we asked of him.* 1 John 5:14-15 *NIV*

Read that again. Do any of you see how HUGE the promise is of this verse? So, the key to getting our prayers answered is to know what the will of God is in any given circumstance! Jesus confirms this Himself when He is asked by the Disciples as to how they should pray, He said, "Father, Your kingdom come, *Your will be done on earth* as it is in heaven." One of our primary callings as God's sons and daughters is to constantly be praying for and enacting His will on the earth. This is what Jesus did and it radically changed things.

There are circumstances in life that occur to which the Bible speaks directly to. When these occur, it is no mystery as to what the will of the Lord is in those situations. Therefore, it is just a matter of praying and doing according to the Word of God. Verse 14 says, "This is the *confidence* we have in approaching God." Another way of saying this is that we can have *faith* that we are going to get results when coming to the Father for these things.

Let's look at all of the other verses in the Bible that this truth unlocks for us:

> *Let us therefore come boldly to the throne of grace, that we may obtain mercy and find grace to help in time of need.* Hebrews 4:16

> *If any of you lacks wisdom, let him ask of God, who gives to all liberally and without reproach, and it will be given to him.* James 1:5

Confidence in approaching God and coming boldly to His throne for answers without worrying that you are going to get rejected or berated for your shortcomings is what sons and daughters do. We should expect good things as we presume upon His love, goodness, and care. But let us look at the subsequent verses that can be a determining factor that will short-circuit these amazing promises to us.

> *If any of you lacks wisdom, let him ask of God, who gives to all liberally and without reproach, and it will be given to him.* ***But let him ask in faith, with no doubting****, for he who doubts is like a wave of the sea driven and tossed by the wind. For let not that man suppose that he will receive anything from the Lord; he is a double-minded man, unstable in all his ways.* James 1:5-8

Wow! If this verse means what it says, then we would be wise to do whatever we could to get ourselves out of unbelief and into knowing and believing what the Lord wants for us, according to His heart and His Word. This is at the very core of Christianity—to know Him and His love for us personally. He longs to be good to us individually.

So, now we can establish two certainties to get our prayers answered: first, pray according to His will; second, pray in faith. If you do not know His will regarding a particular issue, then it is more challenging to have faith that He will answer.

When the Answer Is Not in the Bible

When Jesus was tempted by Satan in the wilderness after fasting for forty days, Satan pointed out that Jesus had the power to turn the surrounding stones into bread to relieve His dire hunger. Jesus responded with scripture from Deuteronomy 8:3, "It is written, 'Man shall not live by bread alone, but by every word that proceeds from the mouth of God.'"

Notice that it does not say that we live by every word that *proceed**ed*** (past tense) from the mouth of God. It says that the life-giving words of God (that we should be living on) are His word that *proceeds* (current, continual tense) from the mouth of God to us. They are current "*now words*" to us, from God. This is essential to carrying on any relationship.

This Old Testament reference was referring to the fact that God had given manna every morning to His people, Israel, for forty years in the desert. Every time they tried to store the manna or bread for use the next day, it would rot and get worms. The lesson: you cannot live on yesterday's bread!

In the same way, we cannot live on just Bible knowledge alone. We must have fresh spiritual bread from the Lord daily through a vibrant, living relationship. Jesus said that He was the "living bread that came down from Heaven." He said that we must "eat His flesh." He is also called "the Word that became flesh." He says that "His mercies are new every morning," just as the manna was new every morning for the Israelites. He instructs us to pray, "Give us this day, our daily bread." In the Temple, there was the "showbread," better translated as "bread of Presence." This was the bread that was constantly in the Presence of the Lord. If you ate the bread, you would be in His Presence, because you could not separate the two. One came with the other as a package deal. All this mystery points to the true bread from Heaven, Jesus Christ, the Living Word, who is speaking to us every day, *proceeding* from the mouth of the Father. Do you now see this as a common theme throughout the Scriptures?

An important note: every "now word" that proceeds from the mouth of God to us today will never be in contradiction with the Word that has already been spoken, namely, the Bible. This does not mean, however, that it will not be in contradiction to what *our current understanding* or *opinion* is of the particular portion of the Bible.

With the Bible so full of these clear prophetic and symbolic signs showing us that God wants to carry on a conversation with us about our lives, what do we do when we are not hearing anything from Him, or we can't find the specific answer that we need in the pages of Scripture?

> *Likewise, the Spirit also helps in our weaknesses. For we do not know what we should pray for as we ought, but the Spirit Himself makes intercession for us with*

> *groanings which cannot be uttered. Now He who searches the hearts knows what the mind of the Spirit is, because He makes intercession for the saints according to the will of God.* Romans 8:26-27

The Holy Spirit makes intercession for us according to the will of God. One of His titles is "Helper," after all. So, the Holy Spirit knows what the will of God is for us in *every* circumstance, even if we do not. Now the gift of tongues is the tool by which the Holy Spirit enables a Christian to put into words the deep things of our spirit. Remember, praying in tongues is our spirit speaking directly to God (1 Corinthians 14:2). He gives us spiritual words that come from our spirit, *not* our mind. We pray, and these words are always in accordance with the will of God because they are articulated by the Holy Spirit as we flow in speaking in tongues.

Let's talk about some examples:

Example #1 - What is my destiny?

Many of us are unsure about the calling and destiny that the Lord has ordained for us in our lives. Because praying in tongues is the method by which we can pray out the mysteries of God (see Chapter 6), our spirit within us can be crying out to God for the preparation and fulfillment of our personal destiny according to His will for us.

Most of us have an idea of the things that make our hearts burn within us. This is typically a sign of what we are called to do in our lives for the Kingdom of God. Some are not even aware of the things for which they are impassioned. So, we have a two-fold problem: 1) What is in *my spirit* to do with my life? and 2) What is *God's desire* for my life? Scripture tells us,

> *... The Spirit searches all things, even the deep things of God for who knows a person's thoughts except their own spirit within them? In the same way no one knows the thoughts of God except the Spirit of God.* 1 Corinthians 2:10-11 *NIV*

Accordingly, since we sometimes do not even know what our own heart's desires are, nor what the plans and purposes of God are for our lives, the Bible makes it clear that our spirit within us and the Holy Spirit of God do. So, what is the solution to be able to tap into those unknown mysteries of the spirits of both God and us? To pray in tongues allows the depths of our spirit (even the hidden desires) to express ourselves to God by the power of the Holy Spirit. Also, the Holy Spirit can cause us to begin praying out His will for our destiny, according to the hidden depths of His Spirit. What an amazing transaction! And all you need to do is pray in faith.

So, the next time that you find yourself stressing out over the direction of your life (or lack thereof), lay hold of that fear and anxiety and make it obedient to Christ Jesus by praying,

> "Father, I thank You for being even more interested and invested in my life than even I am. Therefore, I am going to intercede for my destiny right now from the depths of my spirit, by the power of Your Spirit, according to Your perfect will and plan. By faith, right now, I believe that You are guiding and empowering my spirit in prayer for my life and destiny."

Then begin praying in tongues until you feel the burden lift and peace return.

In his teaching, *Breaking Controlling Spirits*, Dr. Lance Wallnau tells of his sudden thrust into involvement with President Trump, politics, economics, race relations, and media. Upon finding himself in these arenas with other well-known Christian leaders, he asked the Lord (paraphrased),

> "What am I even doing here? It doesn't make any sense. I don't want to be involved in these things, nor have I had any prophetic words in the past about getting involved in these things."

He said that the Lord answered him and said,

> "I'm only answering your prayers."
>
> "But I never prayed for these."
>
> "Every time that you pray in tongues, you're praying about the battle over the nation. You're praying for deliverance for the United States, and this is what I'm doing because I'm answering your prayer to get involved with solving the problem."

You see, even though we may not be able to connect the dots of how we get from where we are at currently (point A), to the place where our next God-ordained level or assignment is (point B) by leaning on our own understanding, the Holy Spirit knows all of those details and exactly how to pray out those details according to the will of God through us, via our tongues.

Example #2 - Who to marry?

Well, the Bible is not going to tell you specifically which person to marry, although it does give you guidelines that you should wisely follow regarding the parameters of your choice.

As long as marrying this person does not violate any of the clear "deal-breakers" found in Scripture, you can then proceed to pray regarding this person. The Lord knows your heart, needs, hurts, strengths, weaknesses, etc., as well as those of a potential spouse. Since you do not know the specific will of God regarding this issue, it is of great benefit to turn it over to the Holy Spirit, the One who always prays in accordance with God's will.

With your mind, you just say, "Lord, I'm really wanting to get married, but I do not presume to know what is best for me, but You do! So, I am going to pray about this issue 'in the Spirit' right now, believing that you will cause me to pray out this most important choice for me and my life." Then, you pray in tongues expecting Him to drop into your mind/heart a little nugget of truth, whether perceptively or imperceptibly. But if He does not, that is okay, as you are praying in faith, knowing that He hears the deep cry of your spirit. Through your spirit language, the Holy Spirit is praying everything out in accordance with the Father's will for you.

Example #3 - Which to choose?

Whether it be which job to take, which house/car to buy, which school to go to, which career path to follow, which city to move to, or which church to attend, there are many important choices in life that we consistently have to make.

Of course, we should initially use the wisdom found in Scripture to narrow down the good choices and find the "God choices". For example, if one of the houses you are considering purchasing is way out of your budget, and you really love it, but getting it would prevent you from paying back the money that you borrowed from some family members with the promise of repayment, then it would go against biblical principles to get that more expensive house. There are so many verses in Proverbs and Ecclesiastes that would speak to this issue.

After the scriptural wisdom criteria are fulfilled, then pray in tongues over the choice. Trust and believe that God is on the job, either narrowing your options for you or bringing clarity to your spirit as to what is the best decision for you to make. You are not an orphan on your own. He loves you and wants to help. Sometimes, He may just say to you, "Either choice is a good one, which do you want? I'll bless either!"

Praying When My Soul Can't

This diagram shows how praying in the spirit is God's ingenious bypass that allows us to pray effectively, in accordance with God's will, regardless of where we're at in our mind and emotions (soul).

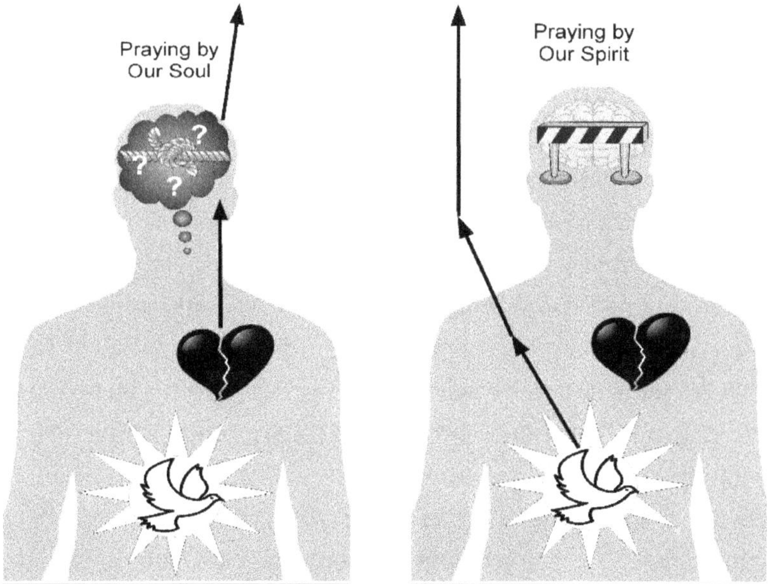

Example #4 - I know I need to forgive, but I don't even know where to start!

In this case, we know that God's will is for us to forgive based on Jesus' statement that unless we forgive others, from our heart, the Father cannot forgive us (Matthew 6:15). But in relationships, especially with family members and those closest to us, there are myriads of layers that have to be dealt with, navigated through, and if possible, restored. Sometimes the pain is so bad that we avoid ever thinking about it for too long, let alone beginning to take steps towards reconciliation.

One of the mistakes that we can make is to think that forgiveness and reconciliation mean a total return to the relationship's previous state before the offense. This can be an erroneous assumption. Sometimes, there are people that the Lord may not want back in the circumference of our lives because of dysfunctions. Although the Lord wants and expects us to "forgive your brother from your heart" (Matt. 18:35), it is important to know to what extent the relationship and communication are to be restored, and the timing of it.

Since these are deeply personal and specific issues, it is difficult to find answers concerning the process in the pages of the Bible. But thank God for the Holy Spirit! We do not know what we should pray, but as always, He does. When we are bogged down by hurt and offense towards someone, but we know that the answer to our pain is in the ability to truly forgive them and to be able to pray for them from a clean heart, we can pray in tongues for them. As I wrote in Chapter 7 (the section, God's Ingenious Bypass), you can do this without focusing on and dwelling on the pain and offense that they have caused you. Through praying in tongues, you can unleash the Holy Spirit through your prayer language to position your heart to forgive and eventually begin praying for them with your soul (mind, will, and emotions), in English.

Example #5 - I know I should pray, but I'm too angry!

Often, we can find ourselves in situations where we are enraged and very angry. Now, being angry is not a sin, but anger can be the proverbial banana peel that we can slip on right into sin.

> *"Be angry, and do not sin": do not let the sun go down on your wrath...* Ephesians 4:26

The last thing that we want to do when we are furious is to pray. But, deep down, we know that it's what we really should be doing. Usually, we have to wait until our emotion of anger subsides before we can even think about praying. Even then, our prayers can be just telling the Lord how what just happened to us was wrong and what's He going to do about it?!

Fortunately, God has given us a tool to help in this situation… tongues. Let's say that I just got into an argument with my wife, and I am so mad that I could just spit nails. Well, I could wait until my anger subsides and probably say some things that will get me sleeping on the couch for the next couple of nights in the meantime. Or I could pray in tongues, which completely bypasses my mind and emotions, putting my spirit in connection with the Holy Spirit, and elevating my spirit-man above my soulish anger and emotions. Before you know it, my emotions have fallen in line with my spirit because I chose to deal with this issue spiritually, God's way, instead of relying on my self-control or self-discipline.

Here's another example from an article about one woman's harrowing experience with using tongues to her benefit amid unspeakable fear and trauma, going beyond what her soul could navigate.

ARTICLE & VIDEO LINK:
Charisma News – June, 2015
"How Speaking in Tongues Saved a Woman's Life"
by Ruth A. Zschomler

"Kathi's Story: God My Rescuer"
Video Testimony YouTube Link:
https://youtu.be/qH3Ogsegf1A

> Kathi and David Byker woke up abruptly at 4 a.m. on August 9, 2011, to the sounds of yelling in their bedroom. Two men wielding knives and dressed all in black stood over Kathi and her husband. They wore ski masks, and all the couple could see were their eyes.
>
> Kathi, believing she was having a nightmare, closed her eyes, hoping that when she opened them again, the men would be gone. When the 60-year-old grandmother opened her eyes, what she had feared most was true: The men were still there. Kathi was terrified.
>
> One of the intruders demanded money from David. The other intruder wound duct tape around Kathi's wrists and ankles, and she suddenly realized they were going to take her away. The thought of being separated from her husband of 40 years was horrifying, and she began kicking the man to get free.
>
> "Stop, honey," her husband said, "he's got a knife to your neck! "Kathi, who hadn't realized that the intruder was holding her at knifepoint, stopped struggling.
>
> Pulled and yanked outside their Grandville, Michigan home to her own sport-utility vehicle—which the men planned to steal—Kathi was frightened. Duct tape was

put over her eyes and mouth as she was commanded to lie down on the back seat. To feel so vulnerable and helpless and to be under someone's control like that was "Just hell", Kathi says.

According to police reports, the two intruders demanded the ransom from the couple or, they said, they would kill Kathi. They gave her husband a cell phone number and told him to call when he had the cash. A third, an older man identified as the ringleader of the group, had supplied the kidnappers with masks, knives, gloves, and duct tape.

The Ride into Darkness

After meeting up with the instigator, one of the intruders, driving the stolen SUV, sped into the darkness away from the Byker's home with Kathi. She didn't know where they were going, what the men were going to do to her, or how long the frightening ordeal would last. The kidnapper drove with his left hand and kept his right hand with the knife over the back of the seat, continually demanding that Kathi lie down. He told her if she sat up that he would kill her.

"I believed that he would," Kathi told *Charisma*. "He had the knife right to my neck."

Up to this point, there was so much trauma, confusion, and disorientation that it prevented Kathi from thinking about prayer. At the point she realized she was totally helpless, Kathi remembered to call out to God. This was the turning point, she says.

She was still in the same situation, but everything had changed in her heart. After that moment, God was front and center in her mind, heart, and spirit. Lying in the dark in the back seat of the SUV, not knowing whether she would live or die, Kathi focused on God and prayed in the Spirit. She was too overwhelmed to utter a word in English. Romans 8:26 says, "Likewise, the Spirit helps us in our weakness. For we do not know what to pray for as we ought, but the Spirit himself intercedes for us with groanings too deep for words."

"It's the perfect prayer because it is from my spirit to God's Spirit without the mind getting involved," she says.

The duct tape kept her mouth shut, but it couldn't keep her tongue from moving as she prayed, she says. Sometimes, all she could mutter was "Help, God." As she prayed in the Spirit, she felt her body relax.

"The Holy Spirit prays for us when we don't know how to pray," says Harold Vinson Synan, dean emeritus and visiting professor of church history at Regent University. "Speaking in tongues is a personal gift that can be exercised throughout your whole life."

This is a gift that is for everyone who puts their trust in God. Deb Kirgis, the associate pastor of Resurrection Life Church in Grandville, Michigan, says she knew that the reason Kathi so quickly began praying in tongues was because she already knew the power that was available. She'd experienced other victories as a result of praying in the Spirit in the past, so it came naturally for her to respond to this situation with her supernatural language.

Pleading the Blood of Jesus

Kathi prayed in the Spirit, and the next thing she remembered to do was to plead the blood of Jesus over her body. She thought about the Scripture from the book of Exodus that talks about the blood over the doorposts being protection, and realized she needed God's protection. The more she surrendered to the Spirit, she says, the more scriptures came to mind, including Proverbs 3:5-6: "Trust in the Lord with all your heart and lean not on your own understanding; in all your ways acknowledge him, and he will make your paths straight."

She thought, "I don't know what's going on here, but I'm going to acknowledge Him."

As God brought Scripture after Scripture to her mind, a tremendous peace washed over her. The situation hadn't changed, she says. Before she acknowledged God, she felt scared, but afterwards she felt powerful.

"The fear factor was lessening as the God factor was going up," Kathi says.

Kathi believes she was given supernatural empowerment through the Spirit. She was still terrified but had an otherworldly peace inside. Acts 1:8 says, "But you will receive power when the Holy Spirit comes on you; and you will be my witnesses in Jerusalem, and in all Judea and Samaria, and to the ends of the earth."

Her thoughts came fast, and she remembered Psalm 91 and the word "protection." Psalm 91:1-2 says, "Whoever dwells in the shelter of the Most High will rest in the shadow of the Almighty. I will say of the Lord, 'He is my refuge and my fortress, my god, in whom I trust.' "

It was then that Kathi realized that God was greater than her fear, and she could rest in Him.

A Miraculous Escape

Soon after, the driver stopped the car and pulled into what she thought was a forest. She remembers thinking, "I am not going to be one of those people who are never heard from again, in Jesus' name!"

Kathi was dragged into a field in another Michigan county where the abductor began binding her to a telephone pole with duct tape.

"There's somebody behind you, and if you try to escape, he'll kill you," he told her, and then he left. Kathi didn't believe he was telling the truth; she never got the sense that anyone else was there. She heard him leave, and while he was gone, she counted to 10 before wiggling out of the duct tape on her wrists and pulling it from her eyes and mouth. Kathi then realized she was in a cornfield with corn stalks towering around her. She looked around and didn't see anyone else. She looked down and saw the duct tape around her knees and easily pushed it apart.

"It was a miracle," she says. "The duct tape that was holding me to the pole ripped as I just put a slight pressure on it." She thought, *"Wow, God!"* It was then that Kathi made her escape. The police detective later confirmed that there had to have been some sort of help from above. "It was regular duct tape," Kathi says. "It was strong and wrapped around a couple of times. It was tied around my knees. I saw it rip after just slight pressure, and it was a miracle."

Listen to God's Directions

Kathi ran to the road and paused. "It's extremely important which way I go—straight, left, or right," she realized. "In my heart, I asked God which way?" There was no doubt in her mind that God was leading her to go straight, she says. She didn't know which way her kidnapper had gone, but she learned later that she would have run into him if she had gone to the left to get her vehicle. She also found out why her abductor had left her alone; he had run out of tape and gone back to the car for more.

No one prepares themselves for this kind of situation, Kathi says, and she had no idea what to do; she didn't know whether to keep running or find a place to hide. She was still scared for her life.

"I never felt so alone in my life," Kathi says. "Nobody knew where I was. Nobody."

She ran behind a farmhouse in the dark, barefoot and in her stretchy leopard print pajamas, duct tape hanging all over her. Sometimes she stopped to hide and pray, like inside the 3-by-4 metal box she came upon. Other times, she just ran for her life, zigzagging behind whatever she thought would give her cover in the dim early morning light.

At last, in front of a building, she saw a sign in the distance that read, "Classic Transportation." God kept directing her eyes to the sign, and she told herself to remember it. As she prayed, God clearly told her to go closer, where she saw a 12-foot chain link fence with white semitrucks lined up inside. "I was so happy the gate was open," Kathi says.

She hurried past the darkened trucks until she saw one lone red truck with the parking lights on and the engine running. She assumed someone was inside and banged on the truck, but nobody answered. She was relieved to find the driver's side door unlocked and cautiously opened it before softly calling in to a man who had been sleeping in the back.

"Can you help me?" she cried. "I have been kidnapped."

At first, he was in a state of disbelief. But after hearing Kathi's desperate story, the driver called the local police in Allegan County. While they waited, he explained that he was waiting for Classic Transportation to open so he could apply for a job. "He had never been there before, and I felt God had put him there to help me," Kathi says. "I told him, 'I think you're an angel,' and he laughed."

Afterward, the police came and took her to the rural police station, where she retold the events of that night. After that, since the kidnappers had crossed county lines, the Grandville police arrived and questioned her again. "I just praised God that I was a witness to His power," Kathi says.

Prayer: The Deciding Factor

Kathi first became acquainted with the Spirit shortly after her son's birth three decades ago. At the time in 1984, her son was just three months old. She had attended church for many years but always felt something was missing and was searching for more. It was then that a friend told her about the baptism of the Holy Spirit, laid hands on her, and prayed. "I was filled with the love and knowledge of God," Kathi says. She then began voraciously studying Scripture and underlining all the verses about the Holy Spirit. She came to the verse in Ephesians 4:30 that says *Don't grieve the Spirit.* "God said I was resisting the part about speaking in tongues," she says. "But He waited until I was ready."

Kathi was happy praising God in English, and anything more was out of her realm of understanding. She wasn't open to praying in tongues until she realized she was grieving the Spirit and repented. It was only after that that she let herself be open to speaking in tongues. Her prayer language began with only one word but has gradually grown as she has opened herself up to the power of the Spirit.

Doug Bergsma, 63, pastor of Rockford Resurrection Life Church in Rockford, Michigan, has known the Bykers for more than 20 years. When Kathi was kidnapped, Bergsma, who considers himself a straight-line Bible teacher who believes in the gifts of the Spirit, was one of the people David called. Bergsma immediately prayed. By the time he arrived at the Byker's home, there were nearly a dozen people already gathered, praying, some in tongues, and claiming Scripture for Kathi.

He explains that when you are baptized with the Holy Spirit, you get a prayer language: the ability to speak in another language. In 1 Corinthians 14:15, Paul says, "What is it then? I will pray with the spirit, and I will pray with the understanding." Tongues are a spiritual gift, and there are so many things that come from that, Bergsma says. "I have seen so many things over the years, like words of direction, stories of divine protection, revelation, and illumination beyond what the mind can grasp," Bergsma says. "In that situation, for Kathi to have peace and find peace is amazing proof of God's divine protection," Bergsma says.

Release of Bitterness

The three men involved in the kidnapping are now serving long-term prison sentences. "Because forgiveness is a choice, and not a feeling, I have chosen to forgive these men before God," Kathi says. "And therefore, God has miraculously removed bitterness and resentment from me, and He's freed me. Most Americans like me take their freedom for granted. When mine was snatched away, even for a short time, I discovered how extremely valuable it is. To be free is a treasure."

God is our freedom fighter and deliverer, she says. "There are a lot of people who are going through things spiritually that I went through physically," she says. "They are bound up. They are being held hostage. The devil does that; he doesn't play fair, he hates us all, and God is there to rescue us all. I can testify He is there at the hardest times we can imagine. He's not just there for me; He's there for everyone."

Chapter Ten

Worship and Throne Room Realities

"Worshiptainment"… Big Screens, Smoke Machines, & Skinny Jeans

I have already briefly touched on the topic of soul vs. spirit in Chapter 8 (p.150-153), *Spirit Muscle*, but there is much more that this affects within the Church, especially regarding our times of worship.

I have observed throughout the latter part of the 20th Century and well into the 21st, that a majority of the most anointed, passionate, and thus most popular worship music within the Body of Christ has come from the Spirit-filled, full-Gospel movements and streams of Christianity. Thanks to the advent of the internet, social media, and video streaming platforms, the entire Church now has access to a vast array of music. Previously, you would only hear the type of worship music played in your denomination or at the church you attended.

The 1990's saw the introduction and mass distribution of the big production worship service. Christians from all over the world could now see, hear, and experience for themselves musically excellent, passionate, anointed worship instead of having to just bear through the volunteer talent of their local congregation doing the best that they could.

The problem was this: if people were unaware of the anointing of God that only comes through the reality of the supernatural infilling power of the baptism of the Holy Spirit, then they would try to replicate this "sound" and worship experience by adopting all the outward natural accouterments that they observed in these videos: stage lights, big screens, smoke machines, the young hippest looking worship team dressed in the coolest clothes, the hiring of excellent musicians that may or may not be saved, large crowds at big events where one could feel the energy that comes from passionate corporate gatherings—you know—Christian cool. I know this because I've seen and been a part of this.

Let me say that I do not have a problem with having a high production value in the ministry, meaning excellence. I rejoice that we in the Christian world have finally "upped our game" in the production of the arts: movies, music, videos, books, etc. Some of those early Christian movies were painful to watch, and Jesus Himself and His Gospel deserve better.

I am saying that because church leaders have neglected the establishment of what the Bible calls the "elementary principles" of discipleship (Hebrews 6), namely the baptism of the Holy Spirit and the entire supernatural function and experience of the believer, we have been forced to rely on man's natural attempts of producing responses and God results that can only be achieved through implementing His supernatural ways. Because we as a people have not known the ways of the Spirit or how to function there, we live our lives by the leading of our souls—what we think and feel based on our knowledge and experiences.

It is to this reality in us that the big production appeals––to our sensuality—we want to feel, to emote. Today, many in the Body of Christ are noticing the appeal-to-the-senses form of musical worship times. Many have expressed concern for and drawn attention to these times becoming "worshiptainment" instead of true worship of God.

Bless the Lord, Oh My Soul, and All That Is Within Me!

Remember, ***the soul is not bad***! The soul is *who* we are, and a spirit is *what* we are, that lives in a body. To worship the Lord with all our being: heart, mind, soul, strength, and body is commanded and mentioned many times throughout Scripture. As New Covenant disciples of Jesus Christ, we're not to be led by it, but by His Spirit within us. Suppose you find yourself emotionally or physically disconnected from God in times of worship. In that case, that is something that you need to begin discussing with Him, as it is a symptom of a deeper issue of which He wants to give you freedom.

I rejoice every time I see someone (especially children) dancing, jumping, running, flagging, lying prostrate, weeping, or laughing before God in worship. *"I'll become even more undignified than this!"* exclaimed King David as he danced unrestrained in his underwear before the people and the Ark of God in 2 Samuel 6:14-22. Pouring yourself out like a drink offering before God, regardless of one's surroundings, is a beautiful and holy thing, and we should ***never*** judge the heart motive and intention of one who is doing so because we cannot know it. That is between the person and the Lord.

However, from my observation of being in the Church for decades, we have also turned the worship experience from an *offering to* the Lord, where the goal is to ***give to*** Him, into a time when we come and ***get from*** Him something for ourselves, which is the exact opposite of the definition of worship.

Now, because of the glorious nature of who God is, when we get into His Presence, we get everything we need, *"in Your Presence there is fullness of joy"* (Psalm 16:11). He's just awesome like that! But I know for myself and many others that very often the motive of our worship times, especially in the early days of my walk, was very much about what I was going to get from worship and how it was going to change the way that I felt in my current situation. It was a moment of welcome reprieve from the difficulties and heartaches of life. I do not believe the Lord finds fault with us for this, *"For He knows our frame; He remembers that we are just dust."*(Psalm 103:14).

However, in the circumspection of my own motives and intentions in approaching times of musical worship, I believe that we in the Church have inter-mixed our Western consumer-oriented version of sensual, "what's in it for me" Christianity with a higher expression of what is possible in the spirit when we come before the Lord. You start to notice this as you press into the Spirit of God for more, especially when you begin assessing the spiritual atmosphere of the meetings we attend, taking responsibility for it instead of just sitting under it and consuming within it.

What You Need Is a Good Bleeding… Bring the Leeches!

I love history. I watch a lot of historical movies and television series. One of the things that makes me so grateful for living in this modern age is the advancement of our knowledge of the human body and medicine. For much of human history, Mankind thought most sicknesses and diseases were caused and/or carried by the blood. Thus, if you have an ailment, you need to bleed it out of you by incisions or by putting leeches onto your body to have them suck out your bad blood. Obviously, the patient would only become weaker as the supposed "cure" just lent to the person's further decline. It was a diagnosis and prescription based on a faulty understanding of how the body and disease work.

Similarly, some people who notice that something is off in some way with our times of musical worship have concluded that the lyrics and the types of worship songs we sing are the problem. They say that our modern worship songs have become more like the world's mindset and are more self-focused rather than God-focused, and any song that says something about, "I", "me", "we", or "us", such as, "I'm no longer a slave to fear, I am a child of God", or "Oh how He loves us!" is exalting ourselves and not God. By this deduction, some have concluded that a shift back towards hymns is helpful, if not necessary, where we only sing about who God is and mention nothing of ourselves. I believe this is an overly simplistic evaluation that does not account for one of the very premises of this book, understanding the difference between the soul and the spirit.

Additionally, this conclusion inadvertently circumvents an essential foundation stone that the Lord has prophetically been re-laying and highlighting in the Body over the past several decades—our IDENTITY in Christ. Songs that sing about who we are and have become ***in Him*** are on God's agenda.

We do not want to hinder or subdue *any* form of love, affection, passion, or exuberance demonstrated to the Lord. God forbid! In my opinion, nothing is too "over-the-top" for Him; He deserves it all and more.

When It's Not the Heart Motive or the Music Lyrics

Matt Redman's song "The Heart of Worship" is a result of a challenge that his pastor had given to him and the worship team to reassess their heart and motivations behind why and how they were writing and performing worship songs every service.

> *"I'm coming back to the heart of worship.*
> *When it's all about You, it's all about You, Jesus.*
> *I'm sorry, Lord, for the thing I've made it.*
> *When it's all about You, it's all about You, Jesus.*
> *I'll bring You more than a song.*
> *For a song in itself is not what you have required.*
> *You look much deeper within than the way things appear.*
> *You're looking into my heart".*

As with everything in life and the Kingdom, the heart motive is what will be weighed in God's scales and rewarded accordingly. But what I believe is currently happening within the Body is more than just a simple heart check about why and how we do what we do.

I agree that at various times, I have experienced this same sense that something was off in our worship times, but couldn't exactly put my finger on it. But, after much prayer and seeking the Lord, I believe that the core problem lies in the fact that we in the Church have been conditioned to be more familiar with living and worshipping in the natural soul realm (mind and emotions) than in the spirit realm (by the power and means of the Holy Spirit). And we need to realize that music is one of *the* primary ways to move the souls of men, whether saved or unsaved.

When people are ignorant of the supernatural spiritual ways of the Lord and how to get "in the spirit", becoming aware of the manifest Presence of God and the atmosphere around them, they then rely on methods that move the soul, mainly music, to then hopefully slide them into receiving in the spirit.

Most people do not think twice about the musical worship portion of our church services. It's usually the time of the service that most people enjoy the most because they find it's the easiest time to connect with God, with music being the primary tool, because we are used to being soul-driven instead of Spirit-led. This is because it is easier for people to live their everyday lives sowing into their soul (mind, will, and emotions… where the flesh is also seated) than it is to sow into their spirit—by the supernatural.

When I was first saved, I became a singer on a worship team at a large church. In those seven years of experience, I learned a lot about the corporate atmosphere as well as the struggles that we as individuals can experience during the musical portion of our worship services. Now, as a preacher, I teach about needing the awareness of when we are solely worshipping "soulishly" only and not in the spirit, becoming aware of what God is doing in the room at the moment.

Tongues as the Express Ticket to Entering His Presence

I believe that every single one of us, at one time or another, has fought an internal battle during a worship service, whether mentally, emotionally, or both. For the most part, we desire to lose ourselves in adoration of and connection to God but feelings and thoughts of guilt, apathy, criticism, lethargy, depression, doubt, etc., have plagued us at the very moment we attempt to turn our heart and mind towards Him—we get stuck in the outer court of the Temple, so-to-speak.

The long-term solution to these issues is to get grounded in the truths of our identity, sonship, and the righteousness that is freely imputed to us in Jesus Christ. But, speaking and singing in tongues is the practical tool that we can use *immediately* and *every time* to go, by the Spirit, directly into the Holy of Holies, where His Presence dwells. Our perfect born-again spirit bypasses our mental and emotional hang-ups and leaves them standing at the altar in the outer courts of the heavenly Temple.

Remember that Jesus dealt with your sins at that altar once-and-for-all on the Cross. But, if you are having trouble owning that truth for yourself in your mind and emotions, then at least let your spirit take the lead and get into His Presence by the Spirit. This in itself will help to get your heart and head up to speed with the truth of where your perfect, born-again spirit is already, seated in Christ in heavenly places (Ephesians 4:6). This is just one way to be "Spirit-led."

When you look at the Jewish Temple, which is a shadow of what is in Heaven, you will notice that the Incense Altar stands just before the Veil, behind which is the Holy of Holies, where the Presence of the Lord dwells upon the Mercy Seat.

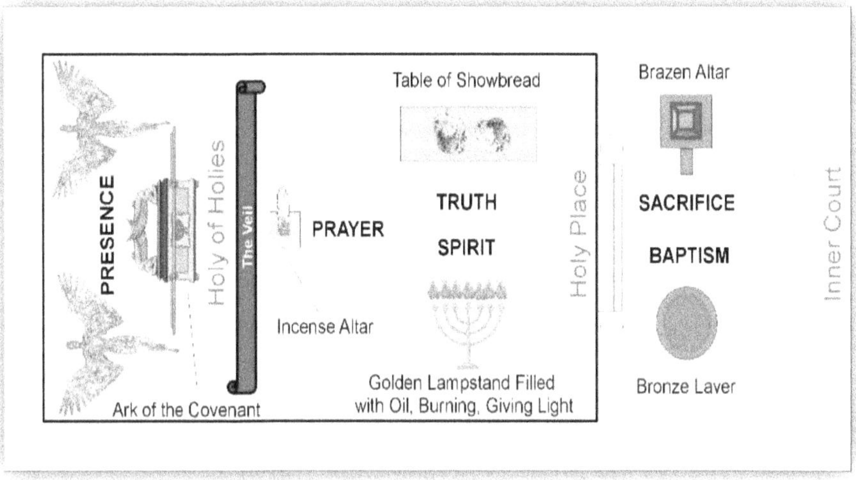

Because we are in Christ through faith in His blood sacrifice and the finished work of the Cross, we are immersed in His death and raised to life through water baptism. We engage in worshiping Him in *all* the ways of the Spirit, which is the oil in the lampstand that illuminates our understanding of the truth found in His Word, symbolized by the Showbread. This understanding then leads to the offering of incense through prayer, empowered by the Spirit, which passes through the Veil—Christ's body—torn for us, granting us access to the Most Holy Place. There, we can enter directly into His Presence by a new and living way—by praying in the Spirit.

When we go directly to the heavenly Incense Altar of prayer in this way, and look up before us, there is no veil… it has been torn! So, what stands before us? The Ark of the Presence! This heavenly language was given to us on the Day of Pentecost, representing the restoration of mankind, with people from every tribe, tongue, and nation communicating to Him in one language: the language of the Spirit with direct access to His Presence! This is a truth that is both profound and simple.

Do you see that even the layout of the temple prophesies Christ, the plan of Redemption, and our access to and oneness with the Father through Him, even while still on Earth?

> *"I do not pray for these alone, but also for those who will believe in Me through their word;* [21] *that* ***they all may be one****, as You, Father, are in Me, and I in You; that they also may* ***be one in Us****, that the world may believe that You sent Me.* [22] *And the glory which You gave Me I have given them,* ***that they may be one just as We are one****:* [23] *I in them, and You in Me..."*
> John 17:20-23

This is truly astounding if we can get this and realize what is available to us. Is it any wonder why speaking in tongues was the first gift that manifested when believers received the baptism of the Holy Spirit, and why the Enemy is fighting so hard to keep the saints from embracing and understanding it?

I find that nowadays, I spend most of the time in a worship service praying and singing in the Spirit. This is not "out of order" as mentioned in 1 Corinthians 14:15-17, as I am doing it during our time of designated corporate worship, and it is not for the edification and hearing of others to say, "Yes, and Amen!" to. Usually, most do not know I'm doing it as I sing along in correlation with the song we are all singing as a congregation. Fortunately, I attend a fellowship where the movement of the Spirit is welcome and most desired, so often the lead worshippers leave many open places in the songs for the people to freely worship, play, or prophesy during the worship set. This is incredibly freeing, and because of this, it is a rarity that the Lord's manifest Presence does not show up corporately.

And finally, what I appreciate the most about tongues is that it is my direct access, at will, into His Presence, and I do not need two praise songs and three worship songs before I sense it. It is immediate, regardless of where my head and heart are. That is the spiritual familiarity the Lord wants for all His sons and daughters because it is a spiritual reality. No massaging or soothing of my soul is required, but if needed, I may additionally *choose* to worship Him with all my soul if the moment calls for it. I do not need anyone else to provoke or prod me to do it.

Rend the Heavens and Come Down? Or…

> *Oh, that You would rend the heavens! That You would come down! That the mountains might shake at Your presence…* Isaiah 64:1

Many of us can readily identify with this heart cry and have prayed this many times in intercession, but especially as we are pouring out our hearts during times of musical worship. I think that there is a prevailing belief at the foundation of most of us, though mainly unspoken, that if we attain a certain level of praise and worship, then the Lord will come down and manifest His Spirit in our midst.

There is some truth to this, but usually, many things regarding musical anointing, human ability, gifting, atmosphere, etc., need to be aligned, and as I've already discussed in Chapter 8 (page 150), there can be many obstacles, and it takes time to get there.

I want to propose another reality to you, which looks at this from a different perspective, the fruit of which I experience regularly myself, and may be very freeing to you.

When we, with a genuine heart, cry out and plead to the Lord for something that He has already granted us and has further stated in His Word to be a present reality, it shows that we don't believe what He has already said. As I get older in the Lord, I find that much of God's challenge to me is not to get more information and revelation from Him about mysteries, but to believe, embody, and manifest what I already know to be true—what He has already said that is a possibility and should be *my* present reality.

Why does He need to rend the heavens? When Jesus's arms were stretched out upon the Cross and He cried, "It is finished!", did God Himself not rend the veil that was before the Holy of Holies, allowing direct access to His Presence?

Why do we plead with Him to "come down"? Didn't He already come… twice? First, as the Son of God, who takes away the sin of the world? And second, as the Spirit of Truth, who leads us into all truth and dwells within us?

So, we're pleading for two things that He has already given us. We have Him here now, *with* us, *within* us! And the Presence of the Almighty should be flowing out of our "bellies/stomachs" or innermost being in power as the River of Life (John 7:38). Do we believe it? And do we know how to access it? Access is initiated to the Spirit by us with the simple gift that He gives all who avail themselves to receiving the baptism of the Spirit and power—the language reversal of the Tower of Babel to the establishment of the living Temple of Zion on the earth.

Break Up the Fountains of the Deep

Crying out for something to be given from above shows that we're unfamiliar with what's already within. What if we're crying out for rain to come down from heaven when He's already sent it? When you ask most people how God flooded the Earth in the time of Noah and the Great Flood, they answer that "it rained forty days and forty nights". But that's only part of the story.

> *...on that day* ***all the fountains of the great deep were broken up****, and the windows of heaven were opened. [12] And the rain was on the earth forty days and forty nights.* Genesis 7:11-12

See what's mentioned first? The aspect that most people are unaware of. The fact is that most of the water that flooded the Earth came from below, when the Lord broke open the one supercontinent (what scientists now call "Pangea"), into the seven continents that we have today. One look at a world map and its corresponding topography makes it plain what it once was. I love it when modern science proves what the Bible has said all along! In fact, today, 97 percent of all fresh usable water comes from below the earth—groundwater. Only three percent comes from the surface sources of lakes, rivers, and streams.[4]

So what? So, how about instead of pleading with God to send something additional from above, why don't we believe and tap into what He's already said is true and available here now? Break up the fountains of the deep! Break up the fountain of ***your*** deep—the Fountain of Living Water that resides in you,

---

[4] https://www.safewater.org/fact-sheets-1/2017/1/23/groundwater

on tap, upon receiving your own personal Pentecost and your spirit language. This is the primary purpose for which it is given!

When you walk in this truth, you are no longer dependent on a specific outer atmosphere being just right or stimulating your soul through music to experience His manifest Presence. When you have any corporate gathering of the brethren who know how to walk in this way, the results are immediate and transformative. You will not need to "work your way into His Presence" by soulish means (which are not bad), but you will all enter in "*by a new and living way*" (Hebrews 10:20).

You are a carrier of His atmosphere within, and He's given you a way to maintain it that requires no mental or emotional effort. Only *do it* ***in faith***, honoring the gift of tongues He's given you by using it for its intended purpose!

Throne Room Worship & the High Praises of God

Someone might say, "Well, how do you know that our born-again spirit goes directly into the Holy of Holies, where God's Presence dwells?" Well, I'm so glad that you asked.

> *But God, who is rich in mercy, because of His great love with which He loved us, [5] even when we were dead in trespasses, made us alive together with Christ (by grace you have been saved), [6] and raised us up together,* ***and made us sit together in the heavenly places*** *in Christ Jesus...* Ephesians 2:4-6

Ephesians says that we are raised and seated in heavenly places in Christ, by the Spirit. We also know from many other verses throughout the Bible that the seat where Christ sits is at the Father's right hand. And where is that? In the Throne Room of the entire multiverse! And where is that throne room? In the heavenly Jerusalem on Mt. Zion.

> *But you have come to Mount Zion and to the city of the living God, the heavenly Jerusalem, and to* ***myriads of angels,*** *[23] to* ***the general assembly*** *and* ***church of the firstborn*** *who are enrolled in heaven, and to* ***God, the Judge of all****, and to* ***the spirits of the righteous made perfect,*** *[24] and to* ***Jesus, the mediator of a new covenant****, and to* ***the sprinkled blood****, which speaks better than the blood of Abel.* Hebrews 12:22-24

So, let's break this picture of the Throne Room and "great cloud of witnesses" down a bit. Envisage this:

- ***"God, the Judge of all"*** - The Throne Room of the Most High God. He, clothed in all glory, splendor, and pure unapproachable light (1 Timothy 6:16), is seated high and lifted up above all else.

- ***"Jesus, the mediator of a new covenant"*** - At His right hand sits Jesus Christ, the Son of God, the King of kings and King of Glory, the Great High Priest, the Heir, Source, and Master of all created things.

- ***"the sprinkled blood"*** - Before the Throne, the very mercy seat of God (whose foundation is righteousness and justice) and before His very Presence is where the sprinkled blood of Messiah shouts throughout all eternity, "Mercy! Let the righteous requirements of the perfect

Law of God be fulfilled! Bless the Lord for His loving kindness and abundant redemption, for His mercy endures from everlasting to everlasting!" The sound of this declaration reverberates throughout the entire cosmos, permeating the very Earth itself that drank in the blood of Abel, drowning out Abel's cries of, "Vengeance!"

- ***"myriads of angels"*** - Ten-thousands upon ten-thousands of angelic hosts crying, "Holy, holy, holy is the LORD of hosts; the whole earth is full of His glory!"

- ***"the general assembly and church of the firstborn"*** - those saints who have died and whose names were written in the Lamb's Book of Life.

- ***"the spirits of the righteous made perfect"*** - That's us! We are there, by the Spirit, seated in the heavens in Christ in the spirit! If that doesn't make you shout, pray, and worship differently, then I don't know what will.

If your mind would be able to momentarily grasp the reality of this truth, and you were standing there amidst the endless multitudes of this great cloud of witnesses (Hebrews 12:1), glorious angelic servants of fire (Hebrews 1:7), the four living creatures full of eyes and wings (Ezekiel 10:12), the twenty-four elders casting their crowns at His feet (Revelation 4:10), and the unspeakable glories surrounding you and the inexpressible things that you would hear (1 Corinthians 12:4), yet all focus was on Him who sits on the Throne… but then… what if… He turns His gaze upon you. What would you do? What would you say?

In the Bible, we see a microcosm of what this could be like for someone experiencing this reality while still here on Earth: In Luke 7:36-50, we see the sinful woman who burst into a home where she was neither invited nor welcomed and threw herself and what little dignity that she had left at Jesus' feet. Her brokenness and sin in the presence of His greatness were too much for her to bear, and words were not only allusive but inadequate to express her innermost being. Frantically kissing his dirty feet, washing them with her tears, drying them with her hair, and expending all her life savings to perfume them was all she could manage. Words were elusive and inadequate. The magnitude of who He is in light of who she was and what she felt, needed something greater than mere words formed from her limited mind.

Whether you have given this any thought before or not, it is the truth of what happens every moment we come to Him in worship and prayer. This is the very place where I realized my absolute inability to adequately relate the depths of my heart, my thoughts, and the need to commit and express everything within my very being, fully to Him. But this is precisely the reason why He gave us a spirit language to be able to express the intangible, inexpressible things of this spiritual relationship.

When we enter this realm, all outer soulish distractions fade away: musically struggling worship teams, off-key singers, stale worship sets, apathetic congregational participation, or self-indulgent stage performing, fade away to the one who is engaged in the high praises of Throne Room worship. Often, while singing and worshipping in the Spirit, I find my spirit language switching into times of declaration. I don't know what I'm saying, but I know that as I worship before His throne, something has changed, and I am now praising and making prophetic declarations by the Spirit before the Throne. I trust Him and just go with it, by faith, and it has resulted in consistently deeper, more powerful, more satisfying, and undistracted times with Him during worship.

> *Let the high praises of God be in their mouth...* Psalm 149:6

In various monarchies throughout history, there have been royal courts that spoke a different aristocratic dialect or even a foreign language in the court, than was the common language of the people of the land. An example of this was in 1066 CE when the English court and other domains of English power adopted the use of French. If you did not speak French, it was obvious that you did not belong in the upper echelons of power or the king's court.

The Lord wants all His children to be full of power and the Holy Spirit, and to be fully versed and functional in the spirit realm because, "it is the Spirit who brings life, the flesh profits nothing" (John 6:63). Before His throne, I trust the Holy Spirit within me much more than I trust my ability to articulate my affections, feelings, needs, or even scriptures that I know. I will flow in and out of both, as well as singing parts of the congregational songs, but I always lead with my spirit so that nothing else will derail my worship time with the Lord or hinder me from having a spirit-to-Spirit encounter with Him.

Bi-Location by the Spirit: On Earth AND in Heaven

There were revelations about speaking in tongues that I did not have until I was writing this book. The idea of what the Bible teaches about the Throne Room realities can be heavy stuff, and I do not expect everyone who reads these things to jump on board immediately at first reading. It's wise that you don't but pray into it and study this out for yourself, inviting the Holy Spirit to lead and guide you into all truth.

This next nugget was something *completely* unexpected, and for me, jaw-dropping! When you have read a scripture verse for decades or even a lifetime and never noticed something, but then, as you're on a treasure hunt with the Lord and He reveals something of value that you have discounted as common for your entire Christian walk, you can take that as potentially divine guidance.

As I was meditating on the idea of us being seated with Christ in the Throne Room from Ephesians 2, coupled with the same description of us there in Hebrews 12, I wondered if there was any evidence that Jesus Himself also walked in this reality while on the Earth. Remember, 1 John 2:6 states:

> *He who says he abides in Him ought himself also to walk just as He walked.* 1 John 2:6

So, looking for scriptural evidence through Jesus Himself to confirm other portions of Scripture is also a wise safety valve, as He *is* perfect theology.

I do not even remember how I ran across this, but one day, I was reading Jesus' conversation with Nicodemus at night.

And there, buried amongst so many other much shinier gems, was this: (added emphases are mine)

> *If I have told you earthly things and you do not believe, how will you believe if I tell you heavenly things* (concepts, truths, revelations)*?* [13] *No one has ascended to heaven but He who came down from heaven, that is, the Son of Man* ***who is in heaven***. John 3:12-13

What?!?

Nicodemus is looking at Jesus in the flesh, face to face, and Jesus says that not only did He come from heaven, but He ***is in*** heaven. How is that possible for this man, the Son of Man, to be in these two places at once—bi-locational?

It is only possible by the Spirit. Jesus had not only the indwelling of the Holy Spirit as we do, but He also received the infilling of the Holy Spirit for the work of the ministry upon emerging from His water baptism. He walked and demonstrated how we're supposed to walk in this life, using the same tools and power that are available to us.

Could it be because He knew firsthand the reality of walking on the Earth as a man while simultaneously living before His Father in the Throne Room, by the Spirit, that He consistently brought heaven's realities to the Earth? Wow! Could this be what creation itself is yearning for as a sign of the End of the Age? That the Body of Christ, we as His younger brothers and sisters, walk collectively in the same manner as the Firstborn Son did upon the Earth!

> *For I consider that the sufferings of this present time are not worthy to be compared with* ***the glory which shall be revealed in us.*** [19] *For the earnest expectation of the*

> *creation eagerly waits* ***for the revealing of the sons of God.*** Romans 8:18-19

I believe this is something worth meditating on and seeking the Father about. The ramifications for us could be earth-shaking if we can truly believe for this, and we can consistently lay hold of this spiritual reality by praying in the Spirit, sowing to our spirit-man instead of leaning on our natural understanding, and stretching forth our hands to do the works.

Angelic Activity & Tongues

In referring to angels, the Bible states,

> *Are they not all ministering spirits sent forth to minister for those who will inherit salvation?* Hebrews 1:14

From this verse, we see that those angels (ministering spirits) are commissioned by the Lord to work with us in not only coming to the Lord but also ministering with us afterward. Angels take their orders from the throne of God, yet will be judged by us in the future, believe it or not:

> *Do you not know that the saints will judge the world? And if the world will be judged by you, are you unworthy to judge the smallest matters?* [3] *Do you not know that we shall judge angels? How much more, things that pertain to this life?* 1 Corinthians 6:2-4

Let me be clear that no place in the Scriptures tells us to command angels, nor to even seek any interaction with them, though I am very open to those encounters. Even though I have had angelic encounters, the Lord Himself is to be the focus of our connection. With that said, though, the Bible is very clear that angels can be a big, yet mostly invisible, part of our walk with the Lord and our ministry. We do, however, get a glimpse from the following verse as to one of the main parameters by which the angelic functions:

> *Bless the LORD, you His angels, who excel in strength, who do His word, heeding the voice of His word.* Psalm 103:20

So, the angels conduct their ministry, service, or mission based upon the word of the Lord, which is a manifestation of His will. In any particular given situation when we find ourselves asking, "What is God currently speaking over, or in this?", we are asking what the word of the Lord in the respective situation is. Many times, we can apply the written Word to a situation by *speaking it out in faith.* Angels respond to the Word *when spoken out in faith*—to reinforce and enact it.

However, if we do not know which part or promise of God's Word to speak out over or into a situation, then speaking in tongues is a great way to align your spirit with the Holy Spirit to speak out the word of the Lord over any situation. I believe that the Holy Spirit guides our prayer into praying the will of God (the word of the Lord) verbally in our spirit language, which angels then can attend to because when we speak in tongues it is our spirit language, "the tongues of angels," according to 1 Corinthians 13:1. I am constantly speaking out the word of the Lord into situations, both in English and in the Spirit, so that the angels can be kept very busy bringing about the Father's will around me. We all should do the same by faith.

<u>ARTICLE</u>:
Destiny Image Blog - August 2020
"What Do Satanists Fear?"
by Todd Smith

I recall a testimony of a leading pastor who told an interesting story about the power of prayer. Years ago, a youth pastor at a large church, along with his ministerial team, had been witnessing to a Satanist and eventually led him to the Lord. The life change was dramatic, and after a while, the youth pastor sat down and asked the former Satanist a few questions period one of which was, "As a Satanist, what did you fear the most about Christians?"

His reply was quick and to the point: "We have seen what is accomplished when they pray. **The response in the spiritual is very significant when a believer prays in the Spirit. We (as Satanists) tried our best to prevent and discourage it at all costs."**

Why do Satanists fear when God's people pray in tongues? For starters, the believer is praying for the perfect will of God to be accomplished, and evil despises the harm that comes to their kingdom as a result.

Interestingly, another Satanist revealed something similar, **"We fear churches and Christians who pray in tongues,"** he added, "We are able to see in the spirit realm and we know when they (Christians) pray in tongues **because we see an increase in angelic activity as angels dart across the sky sent on divine assignments."**

Chapter Eleven

"What About Misuse and Abuse of Tongues?"

I have seen comments from Christians on social media expressing utter disdain for the gift of tongues (or anything supernatural) because they have witnessed someone in a church service act in a way that they had deemed inappropriate, insincere, or inauthentic while speaking in tongues. The typical comment is, "How can that be God? God would never operate through someone like that!"

Well, I never thought that Jesus would spit in some unsuspecting blind guy's eyes either. Or in a mute man's mouth. But in fact, there are three incidences when Jesus did use his spit to heal: twice in Mark, and once in John. Can you imagine that from the blind person's perspective? All you can hear is this Jesus guy in front of you "clearing the pipes" and then "whap!", something wet hits your eyes. Talk about struggling not to take on an offense! But I guess the method was soon forgotten after he was able to see for the first time, just moments later. It takes what it takes, I guess.

Obviously, Jesus always did what He saw the Father doing, as He was led by the Holy Spirit. It is safe to say that there has never been a man in existence who could hear as clearly from God as Jesus Himself. His origin and sinless life were keys to this unbroken connection. But for you and me, the struggle to seamlessly stay connected to the Father is a greater obstacle, though possible.

Usually, our objective is to simply receive something pure, lovely, and powerful from God and try to give it to people without messing it up by getting our grubby little fingerprints on it. I am not talking about sterilizing that heavenly "something" from coming through us without our own special expression, personality, or uniqueness. I am saying that we do not want to mix our "junk," or unhealthiness, with what God gives us for someone else, thus changing what is pure and lovely from God and tainting it with our flesh or soulishness.

In summary, just because a Spirit-filled believer allows their flesh or soulishness to intermingle with a gifting of the Holy Spirit, it does not negate the fact that the gift being exercised is of God. We run into potential trouble when we judge the motives and intentions of someone else's heart while they are operating in a spiritual gift. Tongues is a gift and ability from God, regardless of how the person is using it. Do not disparage the gift as not from God because you do not like the manner of use or packaging. *Because once given by God, the gift is irrevocable, but not immune to contamination.*

"What Is That to You? You Must Follow Me"

Each of us will have to give an account of how we used His gifts as well as the motives behind them. And let me go a step further and say that we will even be accountable for a gift that He had designated for us to walk in, but did not, regardless of if we think that it was not a gift that He wanted us to have.

You should never be closed-minded or reject anything from the Lord because of someone else's behavior. That's like an unbeliever saying that they do not want to give their life to the Lord because of all the hypocrisy of other Christians. People saying this may be correct regarding some Christian's hypocrisy, but will only be robbing themselves of God's goodness and salvation if they allow others' behaviors to keep them away from a respective truth. If it's from Him, you can bet the farm that it is good. Chew the meat and spit out the bones.

Many times, we take offense for the Lord's sake. But I believe that He is not nearly as offended by these things as we are offended for Him. If you are that concerned about the Lord being honored and reverenced in these things, then *you are the best candidate* to step into these gifts and be an example of how to do it in a way that represents Him well. But *the worst course of action* is to criticize the way that others do certain things that we are failing to do ourselves.

> ***Every good gift*** *and* ***every perfect gift*** *is from above and comes down from the Father of lights, with whom there is no variation or shadow of turning.* James 1:17

There is a short exchange between Jesus and Peter before Jesus ascended into Heaven, which I think puts an exclamation point on the final word about the topic of this chapter:

(Jesus speaking to Peter)

> *Very truly I tell you, when you were younger you dressed yourself and went where you wanted; but when you are old you will stretch out your hands, and someone else will dress you and lead you where you do*

> *not want to go."* [19] *Jesus said this to indicate the kind of death by which Peter would glorify God. Then he said to him, "Follow me!"* [20] *Peter turned and saw that the disciple* (John) *whom Jesus loved was following them. (This was the one who had leaned back against Jesus at the supper and had said, "Lord, who is going to betray you?")* [21] *When Peter saw him, he asked,* ***"Lord, what about him?"*** [22] *Jesus answered, "If I want him to remain alive until I return,* ***what is that to you? You must follow me.***" John 21:18-22 *NIV* (parentheses added)

If you are using other's behaviors, that *you* deem inappropriate or ungodly to stop you from strengthening yourself by a gift that God has ordained for you to have, you will still be held accountable for all the *unproduced fruit* that that specific gift would have produced for the Kingdom, had you not been offended or incorrect in your assessment.

> *"Then he who had received the one talent came and said, 'Lord, I knew you to be a hard man, reaping where you have not sown, and gathering where you have not scattered seed.* ***And I was afraid*** *and went and* ***hid your talent*** *in the ground* (of fear & offense). *Look, there you have what is yours* (with no intended use or profit).*' "But his lord answered and said to him, 'You wicked and lazy servant..."* Matthew 25:24-26 *(parentheses added)*

Demonic Tongues

I have heard several teachers/preachers say that the enemy cannot understand what you are saying when you speak in tongues. This *may* be so, but there is no biblical evidence to back up this claim. It is pure conjecture on anyone's part.

I would be remiss if I did not mention that there is, in fact, such a thing as demonic tongues. It seems logical that if there are "the tongues of angels" (1 Corinthians 13:1), then there are also the tongues of demons. Whether it is their own separate language or just one overall spirit language, there is nowhere in Scripture to either prove or refute whether this is so or not. There is no need to delve into this subject much further, as it is not necessary knowledge when confronting demons in the deliverance ministry.

What I have noticed is that when a demon manifests through someone, the demon can become agitated when you begin speaking in tongues. This seems to make sense that if you are praying/praising or prophesying in a spirit language the demon can sense, if not outright understand, that what you are praying or proclaiming by the Spirit would disturb the demon. It may also be that they just sense the rising of your spirit-man, and that is exactly what has the authority in Christ to drive them out. Remember, though, speaking in tongues is for us, strengthening ourselves and maintaining a flow with the Holy Spirit. We are to cast demons out using our known language, i.e., English, Spanish, etc., not tongues.

There are some of you who, upon hearing that there is such a thing as demonic tongues, said in your mind, "That's it, I'm not even going there at all with tongues then!" Well, my brothers and sisters, that would be a foolish decision and an unwarranted fear. When anyone presents themselves to the Lord in the name of Jesus Christ through His blood that was shed on Calvary's Cross to be filled with the Holy Spirit, there is ***no chance*** - ***zero, nada, zilch*** - that you would receive another demonic spirit! If this were even a remote possibility (which it's not), then it would taint the entire ministry of the

BOTHS and the laying on of hands and shrouding God's primary way of empowering His saints under a cloud of fear and suspicion. This is the epitome of contradiction to the heart and Word of God as taught by Jesus Himself:

> *If a son asks for bread from any father among you, will he give him a stone? Or if he asks for a fish, will he give him a serpent instead of a fish?* [12] *Or if he asks for an egg, will he offer him a scorpion?* [13] *If you then, being evil, know how to give good gifts to your children,* ***how much more*** ***will your heavenly Father give the*** ***Holy Spirit*** ***to those who ask Him!"*** Luke 11:11-13

Also, wouldn't you think that if something so serious and diabolical were possible, there would be a warning, if not repeated warnings, in the New Testament scriptures against this?

When you present yourself to God for the BOTHS with the evidence of speaking in tongues, then you can be assured that it will be just you and the Holy Spirit. Let that be settled in your heart once and for. The only hindrance to being filled with the Holy Spirit is *your* ***unbelief**.* And ***that***... you should treat like the plague!

In the times that I have heard a demonized person screaming out in demonic tongues, it has been through active occult/satanic activity, or as they have been rolling around on the floor, puking all over the front of the altar as we cast demons out of them. This is not something that is commonplace or just can happen by a slight, "Whoopsie! How'd that happen?!" This can happen when someone has actively sought to be empowered by the demonic and has *nothing* to do with God's gift of speaking in tongues.

All of this I am saying is from firsthand experience of laying hands on hundreds and hundreds of people to receive the baptism of the Holy Spirit. Yet almost all the accusations of "demonic tongues" that you will read or hear of are from uninformed Christians who already have a problem with God's true, supernatural, spiritual gift of speaking in tongues. Their goal is to discredit and "warn" others about the dangers of it. Yet, these folks have no scriptural stance by which to disregard the multiple pages of verses that validate it, nor do they have any experience doing it themselves. So, please consider the source before burying your "talent" in the ground out of fear.

The Best Defense is a Good Offense

I put myself through college at San Diego State University by working as a bank teller. As bank tellers, we *never* studied counterfeit bills. Sure, we would examine them when they came through to see how clever the counterfeiters were becoming, but that was the extent of it.

The bank knew that the best defense against the counterfeit was consistent, repeated familiarity with the genuine and the authentic. By daily use, we would become so accustomed to the look and feel of the genuine bills that as soon as something foreign to the norm came across our fingertips or a color tone seemed abnormal, we would notice it.

This is the same principle for the spirit realm. If you do not have a lifestyle of living by the Spirit as a part of your daily routine, but only encounter Him at a weekly service, then you should not expect to be familiar with the genuine movement of the Holy Spirit. Also, I am not only talking about doing your daily devotional or bible reading.

There are multitudes of believers who have disciplined and specific times that they spend with the Lord daily, but because they have yet to receive the baptism of the Holy Spirit in power, they mainly engage with their soul (mind, will, and emotions) while reading and praying. As you've learned through this book, there's more! Since speaking in tongues is our shortcut to getting into His Presence by the Spirit, we can flow and connect with Him continually as we go. A flow of the Spirit—The River of Life.

When we are familiar with and learn to flow with Him, the genuine and authentic Spirit of Truth, then when something comes across our path that is of a different spirit or counterfeit, it should be obvious. Familiarity with the Genuine *is* your best defense.

Chapter Twelve

"How Can I Speak in Tongues?"

I have heard some of our brethren state that Christians can *learn* to speak in tongues. This often garners angry comments from others who claim that tongues cannot be *taught,* but since it is a spiritual gift from God, it is only received by supernatural impartation. Well, both viewpoints are true to a certain extent.

The problem comes from the use of the word, *learn.* To *learn* connotes that a person can teach you how to do something, and thus, once the student learns the subject matter, they then have the power and/or ability to perform what was taught. This is true with natural things, but that is not true with spiritual gifts that are given and empowered by the Holy Spirit. This is a question of source. I can teach you about how to speak in tongues, but I cannot empower you to do it. This is what is meant by those who say that all Christians can "learn" to speak in tongues. It is not something that should cause us to get offended. It's good that we can be taught things that'll not only remove misconceptions that hinder us but also give us helpful direction that enables us to receive and operate in it as well.

The Baptism of the Holy Spirit (BOTHS)

The writer of Hebrews says that the "doctrine of baptism**s**" (plural—water and Spirit) is an "*elementary* teaching." Because this supernatural baptism from God has been largely ignored in the Western Church, receiving the BOTHS is very high on the Lord's priority list. This accounts for some of the reasons why charismatic expressions of the Kingdom of God are the fastest-growing sector of Christianity. It's because it is a restorative move of the Almighty to empower His people, at large, back into what He first established as the norm for the Church on the Day of Pentecost.

Here are some rapid-fire questions and answers regarding the BOTHS and tongues:

Q: **Is it possible to be a born-again Christian and NOT be baptized in the Holy Spirit?**

A: Yes. The *indwelling* is different than the *infilling*.

Q: **Is the BOTHS or speaking in tongues necessary for salvation?**

A. No. It's faith in Jesus' work on the Cross alone.

Q: **Can someone speak in tongues without receiving the BOTHS?**

A: No. The BOTHS is the empowerment of the Holy Spirit that enables one to speak in tongues, as well as perform spiritual gifts.

Q: **Can someone have the BOTHS and NOT speak in tongues?**

A: Yes. Although scripturally, *everyone* who received the BOTHS spoke with tongues. One must enter into the gift by faith and willingness to cooperate with the Holy Spirit. It is *not* forced.

Q: **Is speaking in tongues evidence that someone has received the BOTHS?**

A: Yes. Although it is the initial and main evidence, it is not the only evidence. The ability to produce any of the other supernatural spiritual gifts is also evidence.

Q: **Are spiritual character and the "fruit of the Spirit" evidence that someone has received the BOTHS?**

A: No. Spiritual character and fruit are products of the work of *sanctification* by the *indwelling* of the Holy Spirit that commences upon salvation and continues through willing cooperation with the Holy Spirit.

The focus of receiving the BOTHS should not be to only receive tongues, although I believe that it is a huge part of it. The main goal should be to receive more of HIM, in power! He's so beautiful, lovely, mighty, holy, faithful, and yes… FUN! Does that surprise you? It shouldn't unless you presuppose that God's holiness keeps Him from being fun or having an amazing sense of humor. If you just think logically about the fact that He puts such a high priority on joy throughout the Bible, it is easy to see and experience Him and this facet of His character. He made laughing and smiling good for us and others, emotionally and physiologically—think about this.

To speak in tongues, you must seek out the BOTHS. To help in this, there are multitudes of Spirit-filled believers worldwide who can help you on this journey. Simply put, you must go to where Spirit-filled people are to get what they have. Ask the Father to lead and supernaturally guide you to brethren who can help you. Also, this advice does not preclude you from asking the Lord to fill you Himself, sovereignly, in private. This can and does happen; in prayer, in the shower, while commuting to work, etc., but there is also a biblical precedent for other Spirit-filled believers to lay hands on you as well for the impartation. By the laying on of hands is how I received it and how I have imparted it to hundreds of Christians. Go for it! Don't be shy or timid. Be hungry and tenacious. Like Jesus' parable about the widow and the unjust judge, keep pursuing Him until you get the ruling in your favor. **He wants you to have it more than you do!**

Additionally, I have an upcoming companion book to this one called *Baptism of the Spirit & Fire* that discusses the BOTHS in much the same way that this book elaborates on tongues. For churches and regional gatherings, I do a live teaching and equipping seminar called *Power From On High - Receiving & Administering the Baptism of the Holy Spirit*. You may also order the 4-session video seminar and manual of the same title for individual and small groups. See **RenaissanceRoar.com**, **RevivalRoar.com**, or **SpiritAndTruthSchool.com** for details.

Some do receive the BOTHS and *do not* begin speaking in tongues. I believe that this is due to three reasons:

1. They do not wish to speak in tongues, or they do not believe that they can, so do not attempt to enter into it by faith.
2. They do not know anything about it and are not prompted to by whoever is laying hands on them if it doesn't already well up from within them.
3. They wait for the Holy Spirit to begin sovereignly speaking in tongues through them; to *control them*, which is <u>not</u> how it works.

The Details of How It Actually Happens

One very important thing to remember is that it does not take any special faith to be filled with the Holy Spirit, nor to speak in tongues. *It is the* ***exact same faith*** *as it was to believe and get saved.* The Father indeed wants you to be filled. It is also true that He wants to give you a tool that will enable you to flow with Him more easily in a Spirit-filled life, as well as be strengthened in your inner man whenever you use it. *Only believe* and step into it.

This is how I minister and "lead" someone into speaking in tongues. Before laying hands upon them to receive the BOTHS, I let them know exactly what to expect. I let them know that, without a doubt, when I lay hands upon them to get filled with the Holy Spirit, He *will* come, as He is as excited to do it as they are. I let them know that when they begin to feel His manifest Presence come upon them, then they are to open up to Him and surrender. When this happens, they may begin crying, shaking, laughing, or even fall to the ground. When the Lord of Hosts, the Almighty, the Living God of the universe, comes in power upon an "earthen vessel of clay," it is hard to know how each person will react. But however it manifests when He comes, it is always good.

Even as I write this, I am feeling His manifest Presence coming upon me. I know it's because I so love, honor, and value this ministry of the Holy Spirit, it is often hard for me to ever think, talk, or write about it without this happening. I have agreed to conjoin myself with Him in this ministry, and He needs "all hands on deck" to get each member of His Body filled with power from on high. Won't you join Him? I promise you that it is glorious and so much fun to see people wrecked by the Presence of God!

As the person begins to sense the Presence of God come upon them, their spirit begins to leap within them. At this point, I tell them to open their mouths and to ***begin making sounds***. What?!? Yes, follow me. I know that does not make sense… to your mind. "What sounds am I supposed to make?" Well, if I told you, then that would be your mind telling your mouth what sounds to make, and as you should already know from reading this book, that *is **not** where tongues come.* Remember that tongues come from your spirit, not your mind. So, if someone tells you to repeat certain words repeatedly, like:

"She's comin' on a Honda - She's comin' on a Honda -
She's comin' on a Honda "…

Don't do it, as this is not your spiritual language but a misguided approach that a well-intentioned saint is using, hoping that starting with your soul, you will then stumble over into actual tongues by your spirit.

You must understand that the idea that the Holy Spirit will come upon you and *make you* begin speaking in tongues is erroneous. As much as the Lord wanted to save your soul, He did not *make you* accept Him. You made a decision and cooperated with Him even if you did not completely understand everything. The transaction occurred because ***you agreed*** *with Him*, at His prompting.

Many people, because they misconstrue that the Holy Spirit will do the talking for them, will wait until He overcomes them, and like a sock puppet, stick His hand up inside of them, open their mouths, and begin to make sounds for them. It doesn't happen that way. You will be waiting until the Second Coming for that to happen if that is what you believe.

Some people will say that the Holy Spirit overcame them when He just started speaking in tongues through them. What happens in those instances and is not articulated accurately is that there is something like an explosion that goes off in the person's spirit. What is felt is a praise and power surge that must get out somehow, like a bottle of soda that is shaken up. These are people who just decided to surrender their mouths and voices to God in what was happening, and they uncorked the bottle of what they were experiencing by speaking out. God did not sovereignly take control of them. They were overwhelmed with His glory, and they willingly cooperated with what God was doing, and they jumped into the River of Life to be taken downstream. Do you know what the Bible says about wherever the River of Life goes?

> *And it shall be that every living thing that moves,* ***wherever the rivers go, will live.*** *There will be a very great multitude of fish, because these waters go there; for they will be healed,* ***and everything will live wherever the river goes***. Ezekiel 47:9

So, let me address the "opening up your mouth and making sounds" directive that I mentioned earlier. Since ***you*** are the one who will be speaking in tongues, ***you*** are the one who must *do it*. When you are told to make sounds, your mind gets tweaked because you then ***think*** about what sounds to make. Do not think about it, because it's not about ***what*** you are going to say or the sound you make. He just needs your voice to proceed out of your mouth, and then He makes your voice, or the sounds, into words. I know this is hard to wrap your head around because it's a truth that's beyond your head and understanding—a supernatural mystery. But I have an analogy that I use that may help to put this into perspective for you so that you can go forth in confident faith to seamlessly step into this miracle.

The Moment of the Miracle

In the book of Matthew, we see Jesus walking on the water, the Sea of Galilee. When Peter sees Him, he asks if he could come out to Jesus and join Him. Jesus consented. So, my question to you is this: For this miracle to happen, did Jesus then levitate Peter up out of the boat and onto the water? No. Peter had to get up onto the railing of the boat, look down at the churning sea, and step out of the boat *by his own power*, shifting all his weight onto that front foot that would hit the water. That was *all,* ***Peter***. That was *all* ***faith***. Up until that point, there was *no miracle*, but Peter had done his part. So, when did the actual miracle happen? When Peter's entire weight on one foot, extended in faith, hit the water. At *that moment*, and only at *that moment*, the laws of physics and gravity were circumvented by the Holy Spirit, and Peter entered into his miracle.

It's the same thing that happens with speaking in tongues. Opening your mouth is ***all you****;* making a sound with your voice is ***all you***. But when the sound comes out of your mouth, that is when the miracle happens. The Holy Spirit supernaturally causes the words to form out of *your* spirit. He articulates *your* sounds, and you have no idea what it is going to sound like before you even say it. It is truly a miracle and a mystery for which to fully understand must be experienced oneself.

My Experience of Receiving Tongues

The moment that I had hands laid upon me for the receiving of the BOTHS, the reality of the glory and holiness of God hit me so hard that I began to shake and cry. What I was experiencing was such a force of the supernatural that I began immediately saying, "Thank you, Jesus! Thank you, Jesus! Hallelujah! Thank you, Jesus! Hallelujah! I love you, Lord, I love you, Lord!" Now, as you read that on paper, that may seem just fine, right, and appropriate. But I will tell you that at that moment, those sentiments (expressed in English), seemed shallow, weak, and feeble. The only thing that I could keep saying was those three things over and over again, rapid-fire, as my mind could not keep up with what I was experiencing in my spirit. My words seemed like useless chaff in light of the One in whose Presence I was.

That was when I let go of what was happening inside of me, out of my mouth. I was unprompted and had no idea about tongues whatsoever. What came out of my mouth was something that sounded like baby-talk with a lisp! My mind was screaming, "What the heck are you doing, you sound like an idiot!" So, I immediately went back to English… the same three phrases, because that was about all that my mind could come up with under the circumstances.

When I did this and cut off the flow of the Holy Spirit through my tongue, what I was saying in English seemed even more anemic than before. The best way that I can describe how it felt was that it was like I was running down a snowy mountain and behind me was this giant snowball of God (everything that I was feeling and experiencing in His Presence), which was getting bigger and bigger as it rolled down the hill after me and was overtaking me. Every time that I reverted to English, it was like I was about to be completely rolled over by this giant snowball. Running away from it seemed futile. What was happening was too massive, too powerful, too profound, and too life-changing to be expressed in my words based on my pitiful human reasoning and intellect. In my mind, I did not have the vocabulary to even begin to adequately express what I was feeling in His Presence… but my spirit did.

Finally, after about three times of tug-of-war between my mind and my spirit, I just let go and followed my spirit. The interesting thing is that as soon as I let go and just went with whatever was coming out of my mouth, there was no more conflict within me—my mind lost the battle and my spirit soared. Instead of wrestling with God, I began receiving from Him and giving back to Him, simultaneously.

Imagine a mighty rushing river. If there are a lot of rocks or obstacles in the river, there will be a lot of whitewater rapids. These are places of conflict in the river that cause upheaval and turmoil in the flow, which can be quite dangerous, as my river guide friends would be quick to tell you. But if you remove the rocks—the obstacles, then you
have a steady and peaceful flow of massive amounts of water. This is what it's like to flow with the Holy Spirit instead of

contending with Him for control and operating in your own understanding and limited ability.

Not everyone who receives the BOTHS indeed has a powerful manifestation like I have experienced. My wife is one of those people. Although her initial BOTHS was not like mine (a smaller manifestation of His Presence), in her subsequent re-fillings, she has had powerful encounters with the Lord's manifest Presence. Nonetheless, upon her initial infilling, she did step into receiving and activating tongues as her prayer/praise language, just as did all the other saints mentioned in the Bible. It is *all* available to "whosever will."

Discerning Supernatural Tongues

On a few occasions, after a time of preaching, a person has come up to the ministry line to receive the BOTHS… or so they profess. Unfortunately, some people are there to just test you, the minister, and they really are not seeking God. You will discover that when the word gets out that the Lord is moving in powerful ways, it will draw people—the hungry and the skeptical. There are Christians who will come to see if these things that they're hearing about are true or not. "Testing the spirits" is fine and a biblical command, but the key is whether or not they are coming out of a hungry heart to receive or coming out of a desire to criticize and discredit what they do not understand or believe. There is a huge difference, at the heart level, between legitimately testing the spirits or testing the Almighty.

> *Jesus answered him, "It is also written: 'Do not put the Lord your God to the test.'"* Matthew 4:7

Many people who aren't familiar with the realities of the spirit realm don't understand that God brings illumination to those who operate in the Spirit while they minister. Examples of this are the many times Jesus ministered while knowing the very thoughts of His skeptical hearers. The doubters, scoffers, and disingenuous were very evident to Him, as well as how they were discerning Him and His ministry. I have encountered this many times while preaching because it is a thoroughly biblical experience, *especially* when you preach on the things of the supernatural and the Holy Spirit. Our human nature is much more prone to doubt and skepticism than to faith… just ask the Apostle "Doubting" Thomas.

When I can sense that someone's coming up to me with this heart position, claiming that they want the BOTHS, I will always lay hands on them because I will never not freely give away what God has given to me. And perhaps, God may sovereignly touch them powerfully, bypassing all of their doubt and misguidedness, just as He did the Apostle Paul on the road to Damascus.

But it has happened when someone didn't get supernaturally filled with the Holy Spirit, but then began to fake "speaking in tongues" that was obviously coming from themselves, their mind, or their attempt to replicate what they think tongues are. They may be speaking gibberish, but there's no connection with the Spirit of God whatsoever. When they came up, they didn't desire a deeper connection with God and were just being duplicitous, testing me and the doctrine, pretending to be open. This is truly sad and demonstrates a lack of the fear of the Lord, which would never test God in this way.

Maybe it's because I have done this so much or because I have been blessed to have been given the *gift of discerning of spirits*, but there is a ***qualitative difference*** in the spirit realm when somebody is *trying* to speak in tongues from their mind, or they are just releasing the flow of the Holy Spirit from their spirit. Fortunately, I have a physical reaction when somebody is praying in tongues by the Holy Spirit.

When this happens, I feel a wave of the power of God's Presence (something similar to electricity) hit my spirit. Sometimes, I'm getting touched as powerfully as the person who is getting filled, and it can become challenging for me to stay composed. That's just how God wired me spiritually. I use this to affirm the recipient that what they are doing is "the real deal," because I can feel the power of God hit immediately when they begin praying/praising in tongues. It is pretty incredible and so helpful in ministering, yet it can be a bit challenging physically.

Stealing Away the Seed That Was Sown

One of the common things that I see happen after a person has received the BOTHS and spoken in tongues is that the Devil comes to cause doubt about the reality and legitimacy of what has just occurred. This is the enemy's plan regarding everything in the Kingdom: healing, salvation, giving, deliverance, and the BOTHS. If he cannot stop you from receiving these things initially, he will surely try to get you to at least back off from using them to their full effect.

The primary ways the Devil uses to deter you are your mind (human reasoning) and other people. After having a supernatural encounter like the BOTHS and tongues, it is *natural* to begin questioning what happened. But ***be spiritual***, not natural! Remind your mind that the Word of God promises these very things that you have experienced and that there are multiplied generations of Christians who have experienced the same… it has *never* ceased. Let the Word of God be the concrete that cements your spiritual encounter with God as truth. "*Let God be true, and every man a liar*" (Romans 3:4)—even your own mind.

Using Natural Measurements to Judge the Spiritual

There are two very common comments that I hear from those who have recently received tongues, and they are temptations to discredit or doubt what's been given:

"I don't feel anything."

This often throws people off because at the time of receiving the baptism of the Spirit and tongues, they had a visceral, physical reaction; thus, they associate that feeling with praying in tongues. But remember, that encounter was the infilling of power to equip you to do all of ministry in the supernatural power of Jesus from that point forward. Tongues were not the main point, but empowerment for all ministry was.

Tongues, though very important for connection and manifestation, are just one of the fruits. You will not feel anything much of the time. It's a faith gift, remember? But as you begin to meditate and truly believe the premises that I've laid out in this book, you will begin to sense His Presence bubble up immediately as you turn your attention to Him and pray in the Spirit, in faith. It can become your norm!

"I have no idea what I'm praying,
so, I don't know if it is doing any good?"

Then that means you're doing it right! Remember what Paul said in 1 Corinthians 14:14, *"For if I pray in a tongue, my spirit prays, but my understanding is unfruitful."* Again, remember, it's a faith gift. You're praying out *"mysteries of God in the spirit"*(verse 2).

Because we are so accustomed to relying on our own understanding, we struggle to trust that the invisible and supernatural ways of the Spirit are at work. But get over it! You cannot use natural weights and measurements (your mind) to judge the supernatural (your spirit); they will *never* equate.

The Lord Jesus Christ paid a great price for us to walk in the fullness of His calling. Do not despise His sacrifice by limiting yourself from walking in the completeness and total power of the inheritance He purchased for you. As each of us will be required to give an account for it.

On Your Way to That Body You've Always Wanted

Immediately after the person's initial encounter with the infilling and speaking in tongues, I often debrief with them by asking what they sensed, heard, saw, and felt from the Lord in those moments. It is amazing what God can do in a person's life and spirit in those brief moments. Often, it is more effective than years of biblical counseling!

After speaking together about the encounter, I *always* ask them to begin speaking in tongues again, and I do it with them. Sometimes they look at me in surprise, like, "Can I do that? I'm not feeling anything." That is exactly my point in having them do it! They need to understand immediately that this is a communication gift from God that will:

1. Not be taken away.
2. Does not require any prompting from God to initiate.

3. Does not depend on emotions/feelings, or where you feel that you are spiritually with God now.
4. Give your spirit a way of praise/prayer and connection to God at any time.
5. Be the way you "get into the Spirit."
6. Build up your faith and inner man.

I tell them that they just received a lifetime membership to God's gym, where they can lift these spiritual weights whenever they want and become as strong as they desire to be in their spirit man. Spiritual tongues promote supernatural spiritual strength.

How about you? Do you have a photo on your refrigerator or bathroom mirror of someone who has your ideal weight or physique? Do you often look at it for the inspiration that you need to not eat that third slice of pizza, or to go to that cross-fit class that you don't feel like going to today? How about the photo that you have in your heart that you look at to inspire you to be all that you are destined to be spiritually?

By the world's standards, Jesus and His first disciples were insignificant. But, in the spirit realm, they were "ripped", "buff", "yoked", "toned", "swol", "jacked", "diesel", "strapping", "muscle-bound", "beefy", "pumped", etc., etc. These spiritual titans moved impossible mountains of sickness, disease, hopelessness, worldliness, selfishness, demonic oppression, iniquity, aimlessness, and mediocrity. Let us do the same. So, grab your dumbbells—one for each arm: one for Spirit and the other for Truth—and commit to building some spiritual ***muscle*** for the King and His Kingdom.

"The last three or four reps are what makes the muscle grow. This area of pain divides the champion from someone else who is not a champion. That's what most people lack, having the guts to go on and just say they'll go through the pain no matter what happens."

- Arnold Schwarzenegger
Mr. Olympia, Mr. Universe

"For physical training is of some value, but godliness has value for all things, holding promise for both the present life and the life to come."

- Apostle Paul
1 Timothy 4:8

~ The End ~

When Words Just Will Not Do

Strength and Glory and Power and Honor,
these words will just not do.

They simply do not describe enough the praise I have for You.

The light You shine, it is so pure without defect or flaw.

I could try all my words, and it would not come close at all.

No matter how I arrange them, or if they rhyme or not.

They sometimes get very close but fail to hit the spot.

I know there is a language I might not understand.

But I imagine when You hear it, it's like You hear Your favorite band.

I don't have to know the words, still, I can feel the adoration.

And just as soon as those words are said there is a sense of exhortation.

The language of Your Spirit, I KNOW it speaks to You.

I try to use it often when my words just will not do.

- **Jennifer Gidcumb**

Look for the Upcoming Companion Book...

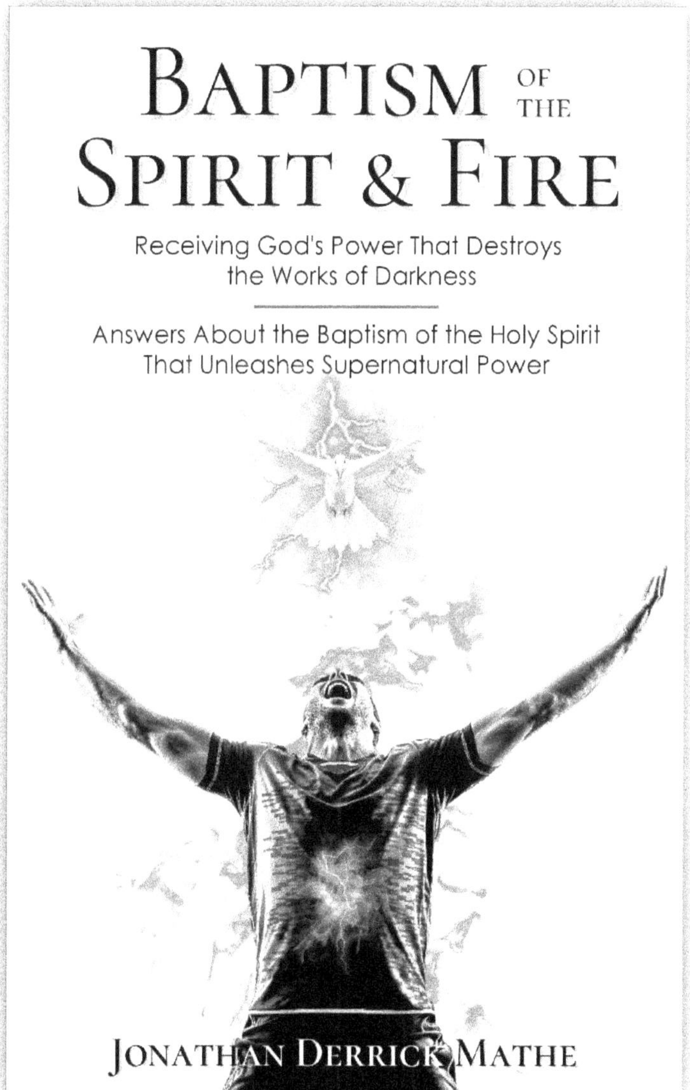

www.RenaissanceRoar.com
www.RevivalRoar.com
www.SpiritAndTruthSchool.com

www.ingramcontent.com/pod-product-compliance
Lightning Source LLC
Chambersburg PA
CBHW071414090426
42737CB00011B/1461
* 9 7 8 0 9 9 9 7 9 2 1 1 7 *